I0105698

EMBRACE

Navigating the Complexities of ADHD, Autism, and Anxiety with Love

Marnie Jurkowski

Copyright © 2024

All Rights Reserved

Dedication

This book is dedicated to you.

If you are reading this book, thank you for letting us share our story with you and know that I wrote it for you. Also know that Andy wanted his journey shared so he could help others too.

With love

Marnie and Andy

Acknowledgment

This book would not have been possible without the wonderfully gifted Suzy Elias and the incredible work she does at the Sydney Energy Healing Hub. She has helped to bring Andy into his light and given much needed healing. Throughout this process, she has become a close friend, and I am incredibly thankful to her for also activating my own light within. My life, and my mind, has expanded and grown significantly since discovering the Energy Healing Hub.

I would also like to thank my higher self and the universe, which continues to amaze and delight me with wonderful synchronicities I could never have imagined. During this journey I have learned the power of trusting my inner voice and while it is not always easy to do, it is – of course – always right.

Lastly, I would like to acknowledge all of the people and practitioners who dedicate their lives to helping people like Andy. Despite the varying success of the therapies and treatments we tried over the years, the intention and dedication of all the practitioners was to help and give kids like Andy a more fulfilling and happy life. Thank you for your dedication to helping others.

Contents

Foreword

By Suzy Elias

When I first met Andy and Marnie, I never expected so much magic to unfold. We didn't exchange words for weeks as they came into the Energy Healing Hub week after week with open hearts ready to receive what fate had in store for them. I did my work in silence, but sometimes much is exchanged without the need for words.

The first time I saw Andy smile, he reminded me of why I do what I do. I will never forget the feeling I had when he told me that he was feeling happy for the first time in a long time.

This story touches all who hear it, and it will continue to touch many now through the words of a loving mother. Words can be powerful, but the energy that Marnie has put into this book will last forever.

This book is a reminder to all parents to expect the unexpected, that it's ok to not have the answers, and that the journey is everything. Written completely from the heart, for other hearts. Be ready to be transformed, to receive something completely new, something that will defy everything you have been taught to believe. This book is the right combination of magic and practical. It's time to remember that we're not alone, it's time to embrace.

Wishing you all a lifetime of love and happiness.

Preface

I've seen so many young people struggling with issues like Andy—diagnosed with ADHD, autism, anxiety, depression, and other neurological conditions. Sadly, this comes as no surprise when you consider the statistics.

In 2023, it was reported by the Center for Disease Control and Prevention that one out of every 36 children is diagnosed with autism (an increase from one in 110 in 2006, and 1 in 5,000 in 1980). Meanwhile, an ABC News article from February 2022 highlighted that over a quarter of women (27%) and about 15% of men under 35 now report living with diagnosed depression or anxiety.

These statistics break my heart. While the increase in autism diagnoses can largely be attributed to improved detection, it doesn't make it any easier. Andy's life has been a challenge, and raising a child with these conditions takes an emotional toll. As a parent, it's heartbreaking to watch your child struggle daily, despite doing everything in your power to help, and still feel like it's not enough.

Andy was a delightful toddler—though you could never take your eyes off him for a second. He grew into a primary school kid who was constantly struggling and being bullied, then became an anxious teenager who sank into deep depression and couldn't function in a school setting. I know I'm not the only mother who has watched her child go down this difficult path. The desperation to help your child is overwhelming, and you'll do anything to ease their pain.

But more than anyone, it was Andy who was desperate to feel better, and I honor him for that. His willingness to fight and try everything we could made all the difference. He is happy today because of his determination to overcome his challenges, and that success wouldn't have been possible without his efforts.

It doesn't take a genius to see how social media, gaming, and excessive screen time play a role in the mental health crisis among children. Though these weren't the root causes of Andy's issues, they certainly didn't help. The exposure to negative and frightening content is nearly impossible for any parent to fully control.

I felt compelled to write about our experience for several reasons:

1. To Help Others

First and foremost, I hope our story can help others. If even one family finds hope or guidance from reading this book, then my purpose is fulfilled. Andy went from crippling depression and being unable to attend school, to finding happiness and going to school five days a week in a remarkably short time. It was nothing short of miraculous, and of course, I want to share that with the world.

2. To Educate

Andy was diagnosed with ADHD and autism in 2020, at 11 years old. I was floored. Just a couple of years prior, a psychologist who had been seeing Andy told me, "He definitely doesn't have ADHD." I had no understanding of autism and never imagined that an intelligent child like Andy could be on the spectrum. I mistakenly thought he was just a difficult child I couldn't figure out. In writing this book, I hope to shed light on how these conditions can be overlooked or misinterpreted as "he's just a late bloomer" or "he'll mature with time" or even "he's just being naughty."

3. To Reframe and Heal with Love

Over the years, we tried numerous mainstream and alternative therapies, all with varying degrees of success. But the real reason I'm sharing our journey is that we eventually found a way forward. We discovered that growth often comes through suffering, and that challenges are essential for our soul's evolution. Once we embraced our situation and reframed it with love, both Andy and I experienced profound transformations. We uncovered our purpose: to raise awareness, teach others, and show how healing and growth are possible, even in the toughest times.

"The moment we embrace the thing that is causing our suffering is the moment that we no longer need to suffer from that thing because we have learned and fully integrated it."

Robert Edward Grant

Note from the Author

This is not a parenting book

Parenting is tough, and I'm far from an expert. It's incredibly rewarding, and I love it, but it can be especially challenging when your child requires extra support. Throughout my journey, I've often felt judged—sometimes positively, but more often negatively. When your child acts out or behaves unusually in public, people are quick to make comments about "bad parenting." I admit, I've been guilty of being judgmental myself at times, and I'm not proud of that.

This book is about love, compassion, and understanding. I'm not a perfect parent—but who is? Raising both Andy and Liam has taught me so much. There have been countless moments where I felt overwhelmed, where I cried and thought it was all too hard. But looking back now, I wouldn't trade those experiences for anything.

I'm sharing both my own and Andy's personal experiences—our imperfections, mistakes, and wrong turns. I ask you to suspend judgment and read this with the understanding that it's intended to help others like us. If it shows one family that they're not alone, and that there is hope, then I've accomplished my goal. And most importantly, don't be too hard on yourself.

As you read, please remember that this is our journey, and no two paths are the same. What worked for us might not work for you, and what didn't work for us might be your breakthrough. Even so, I believe it's essential for parents and caregivers of children with neurological challenges like ADHD, autism, and mental health conditions to hear our story. Parenting a child with these struggles can feel incredibly isolating, but you are not alone.

Meet Andy

Andy was born Aiden Jurkowski in July 2009, the youngest of two. He has an older brother, Liam, who's three years ahead of him and has always been his best friend. Their childhood was filled with laughter, whether they were bouncing around on the trampoline or racing through the house with Nerf guns, battling imaginary wars together.

From a young age, Andy had this flair and style that stood out. Any occasion was a perfect excuse to dress up, and the way he'd put together costumes—fitting whatever he was doing at the time—was not just adorable but genuinely creative. And it wasn't just the outfits; he had this certain je ne sais quoi in everything he did, even in the way he walked. Andy's confident swagger was something people noticed right away. I remember when he was only five, walking ahead of us with his little strut, completely unbothered, knowing we were following behind. A random man passing by saw him and couldn't help but laugh, saying, "Your kid is so cool, he walks like he's already famous!"

It wasn't just the adults who noticed his natural coolness. I remember one day at school, trying to pick Andy out from a sea of kids, all dressed in the same uniform. I turned to one of Liam's friends and said, "I can't seem to spot Andy."

Without hesitation, his friend pointed, "There he is."

I was amazed and asked, "How did you pick him out so fast?"

He just grinned and said, "Easy. No one else has that cool walk."

Andy was the kind of kid who could either have me laughing or crying—there was no in-between. When he had us laughing, it was because of his creativity and quirky sense of humor, often entertaining us with his dancing. He could dance for hours, and honestly, he was really good. Like, really good. But when he brought me to tears, it was usually because of something I just couldn't wrap my head around, like the time he shredded a pillow and spread feathers all over the garden—turning cleanup into an impossible task, or one of the

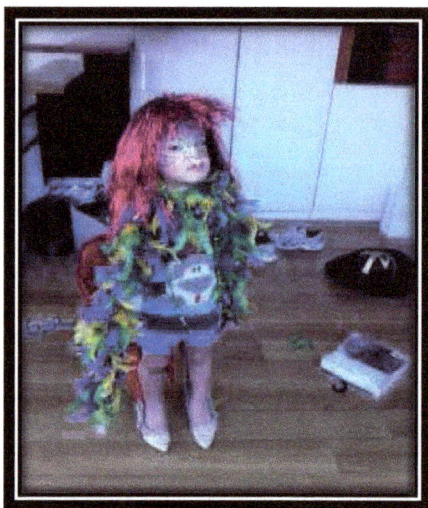

It was very entertaining when Andy found my friend's dress up box

countless times he would steal a random item when visiting a friend.

Despite his wild moments, Andy has always had a kind and caring heart, especially when it comes to dogs. Anytime he saw a furry friend, we'd have to stop while he said hello. He'd often strike up a conversation with the owner, asking about the dog's name and breed, and telling them all about our own dog, Cookie.

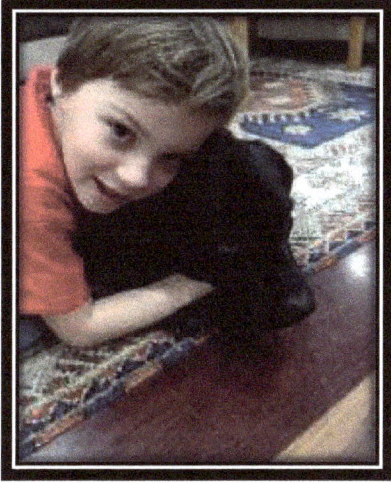
Andy and Cookie

Andy got to know all the dogs in the neighborhood—and by extension, their owners. On walks, people would often smile and say hello to him. I'd ask, "How do you know her?" and he'd casually reply, "She owns *Buddy, the staffy.*"

While Andy has always struggled socially, it's fascinating how he has this natural way with people. Beneath his neurological challenges and the social anxiety, he experiences around peers, he's an incredibly sensitive and loving soul. One example of this is when we'd visit my parents with all the family around—cousins playing, running around loudly—and my grandmother would wake up from her nap to join us in the living room. It was always Andy who noticed her first. He'd rush over, gently lead her to us, help her sit down, and make sure she was comfortable.

Andy's generosity is unhesitating and pure. He rarely has much money (I can't give him too much because he's sensitive to sugar and spends it all on junk food), but when he does, he's quick to share. One Sunday, I gave him some money for lunch while he was at band practice. He bought himself a hot chocolate, and when a homeless man asked for some change, Andy realized he only had his Spriggy card. So, instead of giving money, he bought the man a hot chocolate too. When he told me later, I said, "Oh Andy! That's such a kind and generous thing to do." He just looked at me, confused, and said, "But wouldn't you do the same? Of course, I bought him a hot chocolate. I had money, and he didn't."

"Average" was never meant to be in Andy's life; he's a boy of extremes. If he's not filling my heart with joy and laughter, he's likely making me cry in frustration. He's amazing with people but has a hard time making and keeping friends. He's deeply generous, but because of his impulse control issues, he sometimes steals.

As I share our story and the experiences of parenting this complex and beautiful soul, we'll explore why he is the way he is, and how we've learned to understand and manage him. It's been a bumpy road, but always an upward one, as we've found our way toward healing.

Part 1:
Growing Pains

Chapter 1

The early days

I never knew love could be so strong, so all-encompassing, that nothing would ever come before my beautiful baby. I remember holding our firstborn son for the first time, completely in awe, overwhelmed with love. Tears would roll down my face as I held him, unable to believe this little person was ours. Becoming a mother gave me a whole new appreciation for my own mum, and at the young age of 30, I finally understood just how much my parents loved me.

I loved being a mum, and Liam was an absolute joy—like an angel sent straight from heaven. He was everything to us and brought so much happiness and fulfillment into our lives. One day, I was watching him play and thought, "He looks a little lonely. Wouldn't it be nice if he had a sibling?"

Six months of trying later, and still no luck, we visited our acupuncturist. A few needles here, a bit of moxibustion (which smelled like something suspiciously herbal), and within a month, Andy was officially cooking in the proverbial oven.

When the baby was due, my parents came to stay with us to look after Liam. As my contractions started, we were all sitting around the kitchen table. I said goodbye to Liam, telling him, "I'm just going to go get your brother," and my husband and I left for the hospital.

Andy's birth was quick and natural. One of the perks of a drug-free birth is that you can head home after just a couple of hours of observation. We left the house at 4pm and were back home a little after midnight.

When Liam woke up the next morning, there was his baby brother.

"My baby," he said sweetly, wrapping his little arms protectively around Andy.

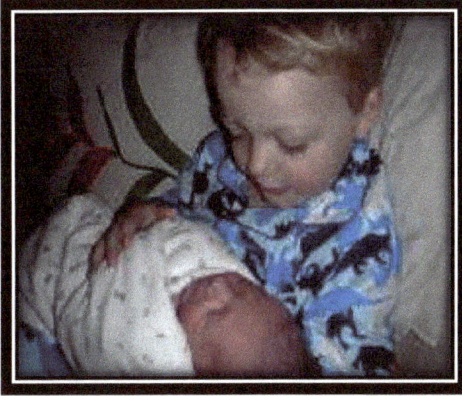

Liam meets his baby brother

Did I say Liam was an angel? Upon reflection, I must've been thinking of the later weeks. In the beginning, Liam had reflux, which basically meant constant baby vomit and endless crying. But once we got that sorted, he really did shine like an angel... all the way through to his teenage years.

Andy, though—Andy was an angel from day one. By the time he came along, I'd already gone through the steep learning curve and anxiety of figuring everything out with Liam, so with Andy, I was much more relaxed and confident. I absolutely loved every minute of those early months. Andy slept... and slept... and then slept some more. Not even Liam running up and down the hallway shouting, "Wake up, Andy!" could disturb him. This kid could've slept through World War III. He cried once a day, and that was after his bath, but a quick singalong of "Galump Went the Little Green Frog" would calm him right down. Easy.

But beware the easy babies.

Once Andy could walk, that was the end of "easy" for him—and I don't think I've ever used the word "easy" and "Andy" in the same sentence since.

Chapter 2

Key Events in Toddler Years

Oh Andy

Andy was a little adventurer from the moment he could move. At family gatherings or with friends, whenever I realized he wasn't in eyesight, it was never a case of, "Oh, he's probably just playing somewhere, he'll be fine." Inevitably, we'd find him doing something like sticking his hands in a toilet bowl or gleefully pulling every single tissue out of a box. My family even had a saying: "Oh, Andy!"—because that's exactly what you'd hear whenever he was found.

As I was writing this, a friend reminded me of "that time when Andy was 10 years old and tried to buy alcohol wearing his school uniform with money he had stolen from his dad's wallet." Everyone seems to have an Andy story.

Eating dirt

I like order and control. Neatness, predictability—I'm the type of person who makes lists and gets real satisfaction from ticking off completed tasks. I constantly have to remind myself to relax, let the kids play, and allow them to get dirty before I swoop in to start cleaning up behind them.

Andy, on the other hand, loved eating dirt. We had a lovely little garden in our courtyard, with jasmine growing to frame the window. The garden bed was just the right height for a wobbly, learning-to-walk toddler to hold onto as he grabbed handfuls of dirt and gleefully shoved them into his mouth. I'd swoop in, dust off his hands and face, and tell him, "We don't eat dirt, Andy." My husband eventually had to cover the garden with gauze to keep those little hands from digging in there.

I sometimes wonder if that's what contributed to his gut health issues later on. Years down the line, we saw a naturopath who discovered Andy had high levels of toxic metals in his system. I can't help but think it was all that dirt—likely containing lead or other toxic elements—that caused the problem.

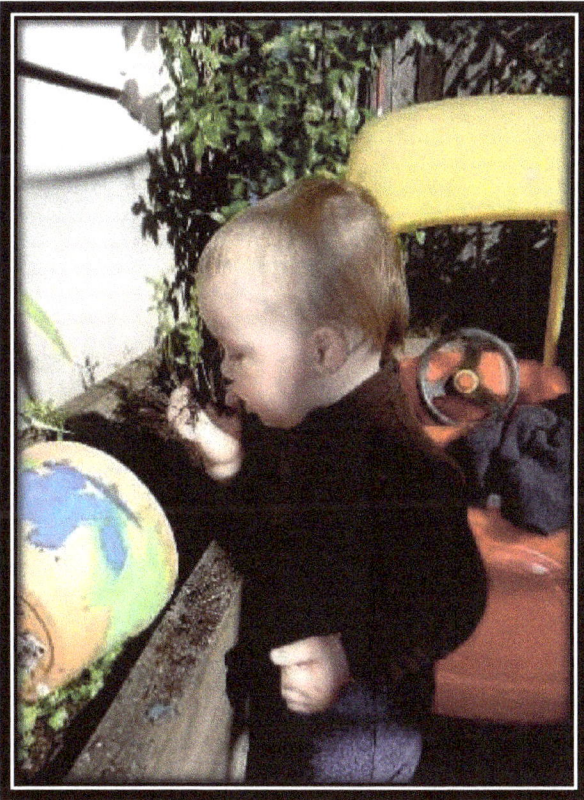

Baby Andy eating dirt

Gut health sensitivity

One of the things I have learned is how common it is for children with autism to have gut health issues. Having a sensitive gut can impact behavior, mood and gastrointestinal functioning. Andy was always highly sensitive to sugar. If I gave both Liam and Andy an identical treat, Liam would be absolutely fine, while Andy's behavior would go off the scales!

Oh, and by the way—I am Batman.

Watching Andy play was always entertaining. He was such an imaginative kid, fully committing to any character he decided to be. His dress-up game was on another level—creative, cool, and so uniquely him. Imaginative play wasn't just about pretending to be someone; for Andy, he became that someone.

EMBRACE

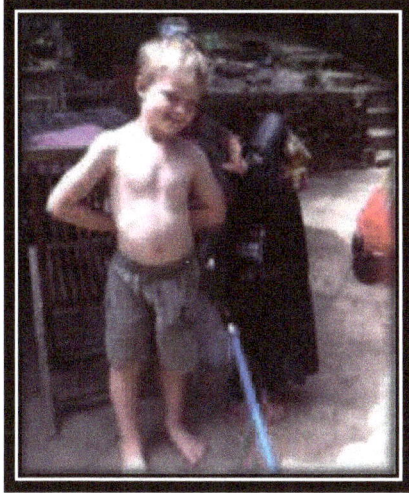

Using the force on his brother

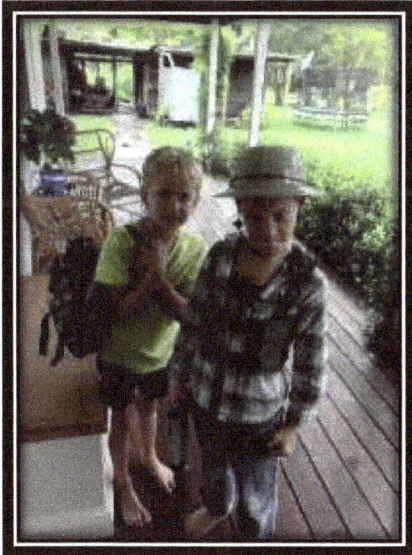

*Andy never passed up an opportunity to
dress up, finding some props on a visit to
his cousin's*

Chapter 3

Pre-school years

Andy was never the popular kid—he usually had only one or two friends, and they were often girls. I think this had a lot to do with his style of play. He was never really into sports, cars, or typical boy stuff. Instead, Andy was all about imaginative play, more similar to how girls tend to play. This has been his way throughout his entire school life, even now.

At preschool, he didn't have many friends and was a bit of a loner. He didn't come across as obviously autistic; he just seemed a bit aloof. I think he liked the idea of having friends but struggled to connect with them. Talking to other kids was tough for him because he didn't share their interests. Unfortunately, this inability to connect became a bigger issue as he moved through primary school.

This was in stark contrast to Liam, who was Mr. Popular and made close friendships with ease.

Bully beacon

There's something that has always astounded me, and it truly breaks my heart for Andy and kids like him. Andy has always been a good-looking little boy, so there's nothing about his appearance that would draw negative attention from others. Yet, despite his adorable looks, it feels like there's an invisible "bully beacon" on his head that some kids just can't resist. I've witnessed it happen right in front of me.

One day, we went to our local club to meet up with some friends and their kids. We chose this spot because it had a lovely grassy area where the children could play while the adults relaxed with drinks and food. It seemed like the perfect setup for a laid-back afternoon.

As the kids started running around, a boy slightly younger than Andy suddenly took a dislike to him. He was awful—pushing Andy around and being mean. I couldn't believe my eyes! Why did he single out my Andy? It's like bullies have a sixth sense for kids who won't fight back.

We didn't stay long.

Looking back, it's clear there were so many indicators of autism in Andy—but nobody ever suggested we get him assessed. It makes me realize that while teachers may not be trained in this area (and it's not really their job), they have so many interactions with kids that I thought they'd be more aware of the signs than a parent with limited experience. Our GP noticed his "difficult behavior and terrible sleeping" but took a rather casual approach, suggesting I just parent him more strictly and give him Phenergan to help him sleep.

In his early years, behavior wasn't a huge issue, but I often found myself frustrated and in tears as he struggled to listen or do simple things like put on his shoes or get dressed. I never considered this a developmental issue; I just thought he was being stubborn and that it was easier to dress him myself than to ask him 50 times.

One day, I arrived late to daycare with Andy, tears streaming down my face from frustration because getting him ready had been impossible. The teacher sternly told me, "You're the mother; you just need to be stricter with him." (This was a common theme of advice for years.)

Having Liam first probably set my expectations sky high for Andy. Liam was super obedient—he absolutely hated getting in trouble and would be devastated if anyone was angry with him. He was quick to learn, intelligent, popular, and an all-around great kid. Poor Andy had a ridiculously high bar to meet. Unlike Liam, Andy never seemed to care what others thought of him; getting in trouble didn't faze him at all. He simply ignored it. I eventually realized that if I treated him like a special needs kid and spoke really slowly and clearly, he'd actually listen. You'd think that would be a lightbulb moment for me, but it didn't quite register.

As Andy grew, we quickly learned he was the kind of little boy you couldn't take your eyes off for even a second. Honestly, I don't know how he survived to become a teenager. We lost him EVERYWHERE. You name the place—we lost him there. He was like Houdini!

When Andy was still in diapers but old enough to run around— about two years old—a close friend with a two-year-old suggested we meet up for shopping. "Let's meet at the mall next to my place; there's a playground for the kids to play in while we catch up over coffee," she said.

"Great! I'll see you there."

We made our way to the fenced-off playground, and I went to grab some coffees. "I'll watch the kids!" my friend confidently called out.

By the time I returned with the coffees, she was beside herself. "I've lost Andy! He must have run right past me; I was standing right in front of the gate. I don't know how he managed to escape!"

After a frantic few minutes (which always feel like hours), we spotted him coming down the escalators back to our level!

That's the amazing thing about Andy—he always turned up. Thank goodness!

We ended up buying him a cute little monkey backpack with a tail that acts as a handle for parents. Yes, you heard that right—a baby version of a leash. Still, I could write an entire chapter—no, a whole book—about losing him. Here are some of the more memorable (but should really be repressed) experiences:

- June 2014: 5 years old: Hawaii Waikiki Beach – We waited until Andy was 5 years old before taking our first overseas family holiday, so we could do things like eat in a restaurant without having to run around after a crazy toddler. We were at the beach and what-do-you-know….. No Andy. What do you do when you lose a 5-year-old in a foreign country?! Run around anxiously looking around the streets heading towards our hotel. When we arrived at the hotel we frantically asked reception "have you seen our little boy?" "Oh yes, a little boy was in here he went to the elevators." There was Andy, waiting at the door to our hotel room.

- October 2015: 6 years old: Gold Coast Burleigh Beach – a beautiful sunny day during school holidays, Burleigh beach was the place to be, people everywhere and of course, crowded. We had been holidaying with my sister and her children on the Gold Coast. We were walking along the grass towards the beach and Andy disappears. Vanishes into thin air. My sister, husband and I split up, check toilets, check everywhere. Calling his name – all the other kids joined in the search. My heart sank as I found a pair of shorts, the swimmers he was wearing, lying on the grass. Oh shit shit shit. About 5 minutes later – Andy turns up (common pair of shorts from Kmart I suppose).

- Nov 2017: 8 years old: Salamanca Markets, Hobart – the markets are heaving this Sunday morning in Hobart. It was so crowded the only way to move around was to shuffle along with the crowd. I had him right next to me, my eyes caught a nice bag/dress/something for a moment and I turned back around and ....no Andy. Gone. Shit shit shit! My husband and I spent half an hour going separate ways to try and find him and eventually we went back to our parked hire car a few blocks away and there was Andy. Waiting by the car. Shit!

The homing device on this kid is incredible. In the moment, I'm often so overwhelmed with worry that when we finally find him, I can't help but shout, "Never leave my side! Don't run off!"

Looking back with the benefit of hindsight and a better understanding of autism (all these disappearing acts happened before his diagnosis), I can clearly see that these were moments of Andy struggling with the chaos of crowded spaces and trying to find his way back to a safe space—like a hire car or a hotel room, the closest thing to home he could find. I also realize now that while I expected him to understand that "you don't leave Mum or Dad's side, no matter what," this requires a level of logical thinking that, in those moments, his impulses completely override. All he could focus on was escaping a stressful environment. And then, when we're reunited, I'd shout and get angry, desperately trying to make him understand that "under no circumstances do you run off." Years of learning how to understand him have shown me that getting angry and shouting only adds to his stress.

As a young child, Andy was incredibly adorable, funny, and quirky. He had an amazing ability to live in the moment. One beautiful example of this happened after a bit of rain at a local dog park. Andy was running around with all the dogs, rolling and splashing in the puddles. He was chasing and being chased by the dogs, acting like one of them and having a blast. It was hilarious to watch! I even have a video of our dog just observing Andy play (you'd expect it to be the other way around). In contrast, Liam was always a thinker—he'd carefully consider his actions and would feel too self-conscious to play like this.

The flipside of being so in-the-moment is that Andy doesn't tend to put much thought into what he's doing and why; he simply follows his desires. In the case of the dog park, it's cute and funny, but often when Andy acts on his impulses, it isn't safe or socially acceptable, or… well, you name it. This leads to a tired, stressed-out mum wondering, "Why am I constantly yelling?" and yelling in frustration at her poor little boy: "What were you thinking??!! That is <dirty/unsafe/not yours/etc>!"

"I didn't think," is always his answer.

"You need to think!!!" I'd stress, feeling frustrated. It's not lost on me that many self-help books encourage us to live in the present moment, and we should aspire to be more like Andy. Yet here I am, trying to teach him to do the opposite.

Recap of early childhood signs that were missed

- Inability to fit in with friend groups
- A sensitive gut
- Inability to listen and follow instructions – never listening
- Poor sleeper
- Bully beacon

Chapter 4

Primary School Years

5 -12 years old

Starting School

When Andy started primary school, I was working full-time, and my husband was in the role of primary caregiver. Because of this, I hadn't been there to drop him off on his first day. One morning during those first few weeks, I was taking him to school, and he suddenly started crying and didn't want me to leave. I asked the teacher if I could walk him to the classroom, but she said I wasn't allowed. In that moment, I felt awful for not being part of Andy's school start. As I walked out of the school, someone recognized me and asked how I was, and I just burst into tears! I think she was quite surprised by that unexpected outburst!

Overall, the beginning of primary school was pretty uneventful for the first couple of terms. It took Andy a little while to settle into school life, but thankfully, there weren't any major issues. I do remember being called in for a chat with the school during that first year, but it wasn't anything too serious, and honestly, I can't recall the details now.

The defining horror moment

When Andy was just 6 or 7 years old, we made a brief visit to a friend who had recently moved in with his girlfriend to create their own version of the Brady Bunch. We were there for about 30 minutes—just enough time to enjoy a cup of tea. The boys all ran upstairs to play while the parents chatted in the kitchen. What the kids were up to upstairs? Well, we had absolutely no idea, but it ended up changing our lives forever.

My husband and I have never been fans of kids using technology, and it's been a tough and somewhat losing battle. Our kids never had their own iPads, and we held off on getting them mobile phones for as long as we could. The family we visited that day had a more relaxed approach to tech; all of their kids had their own iPads. So, instead of building with Lego and playing with action figures, they were all glued to the screens. One of the boys ended up showing Andy some disturbing content. Those images lodged in Andy's brain, and he couldn't shake it off for YEARS. His mind simply couldn't process what he had seen.

From that moment on, several things changed—and unfortunately, not for the better.

1. We said goodbye to sleep. Sleep was never his strong point but this totally ruined any chance we had of him sleeping in his own room for a full night. We really tried but as soon as the lights went out and he was alone it was screaming and freaking out. Night lights didn't help at all.
2. An obsession with horror began. I still don't understand how something that can scare you so much can draw you to it. The combination of not sleeping and being obsessed with horror was not a good one. While mum and dad slept soundly, Andy would sneak downstairs and watch horror movies on TV.
3. Strange behaviour. The horror movies affected Andy in that he would do drawings at school of people being murdered with lots of blood, death and destruction. For a primary school kid – this is inappropriate. It started off not too bad but as the years wore on it would worsen. He would also say and do things that were not appropriate. While I don't remember too much specifically about this, all I remember is that I would get a lot of calls from school and I began to feel anxious when I saw the school number ringing on my phone.

The effects of that incident are still felt today, as Andy now has a fascination with horror movies that can't be underestimated. By the time he was finishing Year One, we began to feel like he was a square peg in a round hole at school. In our minds, there wasn't anything wrong with him—he was just a very creative and unique little soul. So, I started exploring alternative schools like Rudolf Steiner and Montessori. I really liked the look of Montessori, but here's a heads up for parents with young kids: you need to get in quickly! They usually don't accept kids who haven't started in their programs already, so that door closed pretty fast for us.

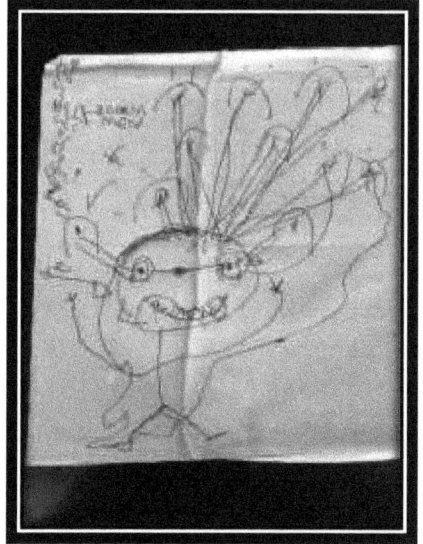

An old drawing of Andy's

Rudolf Steiner

My father had attended a Rudolf Steiner school and loved it, so we decided to get Andy into our closest Steiner school. I adored everything about that school—the philosophy and the holistic approach to teaching are so pure and connected to nature. The commute was pretty tough (about an hour each way in traffic), but we were willing to do whatever it took to have him there.

While Rudolf Steiner schools promote "peace, love, and happiness," they also have a very structured and ritualistic environment. Unfortunately, Andy struggled to adhere to their strict rules tied to these rituals and often found himself in trouble. The pressure to conform to their standards created anxiety for him, which often manifested as him "feeling unwell," leading to frequent visits to the sick bay. At every school he's attended, the office staff has gotten to know him quite well!

During his time at the Rudolf Steiner school, Andy became quite skilled at—let's say—"collecting" things. He would take items from school, which prompted the teachers to suggest he see an anthroposophic psychologist (a psychologist trained in the Rudolf Steiner approach). This was a pivotal moment in our journey, as the psychologist assured us that he "definitely did not have ADHD," but explained that his brain wiring wasn't quite typical. She likened it to taking all the back streets instead of the superhighway! To help him, she suggested a therapy called LENS.

♥ ♥ ♥ ♥

Low Energy Neurofeedback System (LENS)

What it is

Neurotherapy Clinic Victoria describes it as "a unique, effective and safe form of neurotherapy or EEG biofeedback system being used in clinical settings for the treatment of numerous difficulties and disorders."

How it works

"While some forms of neurofeedback use videos and games on a computer screen to help clients develop healthier brainwave patterns, LENS takes a different approach. It utilizes a very low-power electromagnetic field—similar to the ones found around digital watches—as feedback to various sites on the brain. The feedback travels through the same wires used to measure brainwaves. Even though the feedback signal is quite weak, it can produce measurable changes in brainwaves without any conscious effort from the individual receiving it.

During a session, sensors are placed on the scalp to detect brainwave signals, which the computer then processes to extract information about key brainwave frequencies. Using a patented process, this information is sent back through the sensor wires to the client's skin. The result? A reduction or even elimination of symptoms that have previously interfered with the client's quality of life. Sessions are typically brief (usually lasting just 3 to 5 minutes), gentle (clients often feel nothing during the session), and the changes tend to be lasting. However, for symptoms of progressive conditions like Parkinson's and MS, ongoing treatment is necessary to maintain improvements."

Our experience

Andy had about 5 or 6 LENS sessions, and we definitely noticed changes in his behavior right after each one. One afternoon, after a session, he had a playdate, so we dropped him off as planned. A short while later, I had to pick him up early because he was acting a bit off. My friend mentioned that her father-in-law had commented that Andy seemed autistic.

At the time, I brushed off the comment, thinking it was just a temporary side effect of the LENS therapy. It usually shifted his behavior for a day or two after each session, so I didn't think much of it. The effects of the LENS therapy didn't seem to last more than a few days, and while he appeared more grounded and less all over the place, I now realize that was likely due to his ADHD. What I initially saw as him being "more grounded" was actually him being more focused and less fidgety or distracted. It did make daily life a bit easier for those few days—we could ask him to do something once or twice instead of the usual six to ten times before he'd actually get around to it, like brushing his teeth, putting on shoes, or putting something away.

The psychologist also suspected gut health issues were contributing to Andy's behavioral problems and recommended a naturopath. This was a great recommendation and certainly helped Andy in a number of ways.

❤ ❤ ❤ ❤

Naturopath

What it is

The Australian Naturopathic Council describes Naturopathy as "a system of health care which is based on traditional philosophies and principles and utilizes a wide variety of tools and techniques to achieve health for a patient."

How it works

There are many tools and techniques that a naturopath may use to treat a patient, but the four most common ones are nutritional supplements, herbal medicine, dietary advice and lifestyle change (Steel, Schloss, Leach, Adams, 2020).

Our experience

The first thing the naturopath suspected was that Andy had a condition called Pyrrole disorder. She suspected that it had developed due to his high levels of toxicity.

Pyrrole Disorder

Pyrrole disorder is a condition in which zinc and vitamin B6 are excreted in the urine, resulting in a zinc deficiency. Zinc is a powerful neurotransmitter and is vital for concentration, memory, detoxification and digestion. It is required for hundreds of processes in the body. Most concerning as a parent, however, is to learn about the high correlation between pyrrole disorder and mental health issues such as mood disorders, schizophrenia and bipolar.

There is a long list of symptoms of Pyrrole but I have selected the ones I noted consistently as I conducted my research:

- Irritability
- Severe anxiety
- Severe depression
- Significant changes in mood
- Memory problems
- Inability to manage stress

In addition to diagnosing Andy's pyrrole disorder, the naturopath treated him for a gut parasite, and we even sent away some hair samples to the US to check for toxins in his body. The effects of her remedies were slow, especially compared to mainstream medications we tried later, but still pretty impressive. I had always thought Andy was just really prone to itchy bites—his legs were always covered in them! But our naturopath didn't see "itchy bites," she saw sores and scabs, a sign of a gut parasite. Once the parasite was treated, the scabs on his legs cleared up. Big tick!

When we got his toxicity results back from the US, they were shocking. His total toxic load was way above the 95th percentile. He had extremely high levels of lead, nickel, silver, and mercury, with aluminum almost tipping into the too high range as well. He also had deficiencies in some essential elements that needed addressing. I know hair samples can sometimes give misleading results due to haircare products, but Andy didn't use anything except shampoo, so I believe the results accurately reflected what was in his body.

Detoxing is a slow process, but we jumped into it with urgency. My poor boy, at only 8 years old, was suddenly taking a handful of supplements every day. Wherever possible, we used liquid alternatives, but they didn't taste great. He also slept every night with Footsie detox pads on the soles of his feet, which are supposed to draw out toxins while you sleep.

I remember the naturopath telling me that as we cleared up the bigger issues—like the gut parasite—we would discover other problems that had been masked, like peeling back layers of an onion.

Once one layer is removed, another issue becomes visible. We worked on supporting his adrenals, and she recommended removing gluten and dairy to help his gut heal. I have to admit, though, I never quite succeeded at fully eliminating either from our house. I could reduce them, but complete removal was a whole other battle.

Looking back, I truly believe that seeing the naturopath was one of the best things we did for Andy at that stage. In hindsight, we were close to what eventually helped him heal. Detoxing is such a slow process and it's hard to gauge progress—there's no simple blood test or check-up that tells you how far along you are. From my limited understanding, tracking toxicity levels in the body and brain is still a scientific challenge.

We saw the naturopath for about nine months, and only stopped when she moved to Byron Bay. Over time, we eventually phased out the supplements, bentonite clay drinks (which were awful), and the Footsies, as life got busier and the detox process faded into the background.

❤ ❤ ❤ ❤

Rudolf Steiner continued…

Andy's Houdini act crept into school life. He often hid in the playground, refusing to return to the classroom after recess or lunch. "What a naughty boy!" we all thought. In hindsight, it wasn't him being naughty—he was so anxious about being in the classroom that he couldn't bear it. It breaks my heart now to realize I didn't understand this at the time, and instead, I just got upset with him for "misbehaving."

His behavior spiraled downward, and after six months at the Rudolf Steiner school, he was kicked out. I was devastated. I couldn't understand why the school was so harsh. He was dealing with high toxicity that affected his brain—we needed time to work through it!

After that awful meeting with the school, I cried all the way home, and I'm not proud to admit that I was also upset with Andy for "ruining it." The psychologist and naturopath were equally disappointed that the school had turned their backs on us.

I loved the Steiner philosophy—their emphasis on a non-toxic, nature-loving, and holistic learning environment. But fitting in was surprisingly hard. Whether it was due to gossip about Andy's behavior or just the nature of trying to integrate into such a unique community, I don't know. However, I did feel judged, as though if you didn't live the "Steiner way," you weren't truly welcomed. Even arranging playdates was almost impossible—we managed just one or two in the six months we were there.

While it took me some time to move on, Andy never looked back. He hated that place and has never regretted getting kicked out. Sadly, he had also faced social exclusion and teasing at the school, so it's no surprise that it wasn't the safe environment he needed to thrive.

Home Schooling

Since I had returned to work after maternity leave when Andy was just 6 months old, my husband had taken on the role of a stay-at-home dad. He ran a small business from home, which worked out great because it allowed me to continue my career.

When Andy was kicked out from the Rudolf Steiner school, we knew he was on a downward spiral and sending him back to the local primary school wasn't going to help. Homeschooling became our only option. We needed to stabilize him and give him the support he desperately needed.

What it is

Homeschooling means that parents take on the full responsibility of educating their child at home. While it doesn't come with any direct costs, it's important to keep in mind that it's essentially a full-time job. Thankfully, my husband was able to keep his small business running on the side.

How it works

In NSW, Australia, you need to apply to register your child for homeschooling. The process includes a home visit assessment, and once you're approved, you're provided with a syllabus and materials. There's also some paperwork involved so they can track your child's progress.

Our experience

Homeschooling turned out to be the best learning experience for Andy. He thrives with one-on-one attention, which my husband was able to provide. Being in the safe and familiar environment of home helped Andy get into the right mindset for learning.

My husband also kept the lessons short, sharp, and as engaging as possible, making the content both relevant and interesting. These three key elements—focused attention, a safe environment, and brief, engaging lessons—created the conditions Andy needed to show he was not only capable but also eager to learn.

Homeschooling did exactly what it was meant to: it gave Andy the safe space he needed to recover from his time at the Rudolf Steiner school. Though both Andy and my husband found it a little lonely at times, they also had fun. After one term of homeschooling with Dad, Andy was ready to return to our local primary school.

Back at School

After the solitary nature of homeschooling, Andy was excited to be back at school, and for the next couple of years, we experienced what I'd call "relative stability." What does that look like for Andy, you ask? Well, for starters, one day I got a call from my neighbor, kindly letting me know she could see my child walking around on the roof of our house. My reaction? WTF?! ANDY!!!

We continued to get frequent calls from school, mostly about his challenging classroom behavior and social difficulties in the playground. But Andy is clever. Whenever he felt uncomfortable in class, he'd act out just enough to get sent to the principal's office. The best part? He loved it there.

The principal, Liz, was firm—she didn't tolerate any misbehavior—but she was also kind and compassionate, with a soft spot for Andy. He felt safe in the quiet of her office, which was a far cry from the chaos of the classroom. Here's a picture he drew not long after returning to school, a reflection of his connection to Liz and that brief period of relative calm.

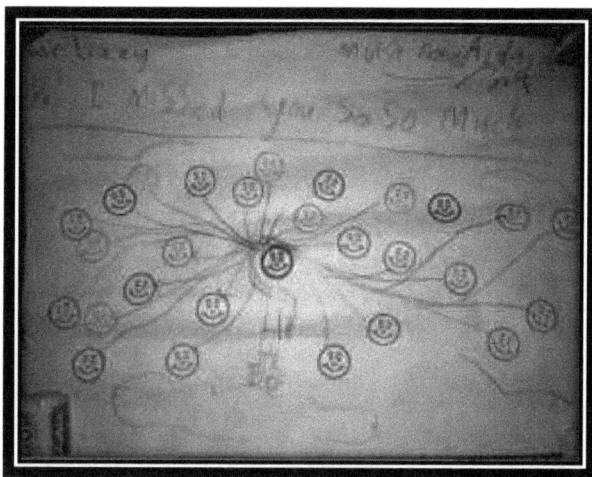

Andy's note for the principle when returning to school

I began to realize that all of Andy's school challenges seemed to happen during or immediately after recess or lunch breaks. Just think about it for a moment—if you're a young child who's ultra-sensitive, what's it like being surrounded by the chaos of hundreds of kids running around, screaming, laughing, and then add getting physically pushed around? Add to that the social anxiety and regular bullying. For Andy, it was overwhelming. He'd return to the classroom completely drained, and then he was expected to sit still and concentrate. My poor baby.

In 2018, when Andy was in Year 3, we took a 5-week trip through Europe. He was well-behaved throughout the holiday, with only one "Houdini act"—which I had actually forgotten about until writing this. Towards the end of the trip, we were staying with friends on a beautiful little island in Croatia and decided to take a day trip to Hvar. After a long, wonderful day, we hiked up a hill to enjoy the stunning view. Lots of photos, a bit of huffing and puffing from the climb, and then we started heading back down the hill. Andy, of course, ran ahead.

When we got to the bottom, he was nowhere to be found. Panic set in. Shit. Shit. Shit. We split up into a search party of three (Andy's uncle had come to meet us in Croatia). It felt like forever before we found him. The tricky part was that we didn't have a hotel or car to serve as a "base"—not that I'd quite figured out that this was his usual escape pattern at the time. We had arrived by boat, and soon enough, the boat would leave, and the sun would set. Where could he be?!

I pulled the short straw and ran back up the hill (thanks, Andy!) to check if he had taken a side trail, or if we'd missed him on our way down. No luck. My husband was checking the shops and spots we'd visited earlier. Still nothing. I'm still not exactly sure how we found him—he just kind of appeared, like he always does.

Overall, Andy was funny, happy, and so full of life on that trip. We all relaxed and enjoyed ourselves immensely. Liam and Andy were the best of friends, and all they needed was each other. It was truly the trip of a lifetime.

Looking back, it serves as a useful insight—when you remove the stress of everyday life, there was very little sign of the issues we struggled with daily. Aside from his ongoing sleep challenges (which sleeping with mum or dad could usually fix), everything felt good. We weren't using technology to entertain the kids either; instead, we played games and talked—totally old-school! It was a reminder that in the right environment, Andy could really thrive.

❤ ❤ ❤ ❤

Back at home, a friend of mine recommended a doctor who specialized in Pyrrole disorder. So off we went to see what he could do for Andy.

The doctor ordered a few expensive tests that were sent off to the USA. Six weeks later we confirmed what the naturopath had suspected. Andy had pyrrole disorder with a side of undermethylation. What this looks like in test results:

- o Very high pyrrole count
- o Low zinc levels
- o Copper in the average range

The main difference between this doctor and a regular GP, was that he was able to prescribe a specific compounding medication to be made specifically to match Andy's needs in this regard. Being more in the supplement category, rather than a pharmaceutical, the tablets needed to be taken for almost 3 months before results could be seen.

We did see subtle improvements once the *primer pyrrole methylation* tablets took effect. Every little step in the right direction helps.

Don't get attached

Andy loved collecting things, which meant we often ended up with some pretty strange items around the house. He had a knack for picking things up from school or during visits to friends' houses.

EMBRACE

After a playdate, I'd sometimes get a phone call like, "Hey, do you know if Andy took or saw where *this or that object* went?"

Think of Andy as an explorer with no boundaries and a mischievous streak. For example, my friend once caught him rummaging through her handbag—he'd taken a few cigarettes! Oh, Andy.

He also didn't put much value on material things. He had a habit of stabbing and slicing objects. I'm not sure if it was due to his fascination with horror or simply because he was such a tactile child. Probably a bit of both. Andy loved touching everything.

For a long time, I was really attached to my things—makeup, jeweler, shoes—the usual stuff. But with Andy around, I realized that if I didn't want to be constantly upset, I had to let that go. I used to get so angry when he'd ruin my favorite or expensive items. Over time, though, Andy unknowingly taught me not to hold on too tightly to material things. It wasn't worth the stress. I've since learned that cheap products and IKEA furniture can be lifesavers, and once you let go, it's freeing.

Still, Andy's behavior led to some embarrassing moments with friends. I could handle a chipped door or a stained carpet at home, but one of the worst incidents was when he stabbed a friend's sofa. She had a beautiful home, filled with gorgeous things—and her sofa was ruined.

After incidents like that, I'd seethe with frustration and embarrassment. I'd cry and wonder why I didn't have a "normal" child. It was so hard. I wanted the perfect family, like something out of a Hollywood movie. "This isn't how it was supposed to be," I'd think. "Aren't we supposed to have perfect kids and live happily ever after?"

I felt resentful that my reality didn't match what I had envisioned. As a result, I acted out like a child who didn't get what she wanted. I cried a lot during those years, and I got angry often, especially when Andy's behavior spiraled out of control.

Eventually, I began to notice that Liam, as he entered puberty, was starting to reflect my own behavior. He would get angry, just like I did. It was then I realized that I wasn't setting the best example for my kids. That was a turning point for me. I knew I needed to work on my own emotional regulation and be the role model my boys needed. It wasn't easy to control my anger, but I did start to change.

I've always been open with the boys about this journey, letting them know that I'm working on it.

a) anger isn't nice

b) I'm sorry I created that environment

c) I'm committed to changing and I invited them to call me out on it when it arose

d) I love them both so very much

Play dates

Organizing a playdate for Andy was never easy. We'd often reach out to other parents, only to get the usual, "Sorry, we're busy." But it was rarely followed by, "Maybe tomorrow?" I get that some kids probably found him a bit different, and the parents were just trying to help their child keep their distance from "the weird kid." Still, it hurt.

On the rare occasion he did land a playdate at someone else's house, it didn't always go smoothly. Andy had a habit of taking things, and as a result, he was rarely invited back.

Looking back, though, I can see that Andy always had at least one friend as he grew up, and really, that's all you need—just one good friend to be okay.

Since playdates were tough to arrange, my husband and I ended up spending a lot of our weekends with Andy. We'd go on bushwalks or take long walks with him and the dog, then grab lunch at a café. Those outings became our routine and a way to fill the gaps where playdates might have been.

Chapter 5

Challenges in Year 4

In early 2019, as Year 4 kicked off and Andy turned 10, his Houdini act started making a regular comeback at school. His older brother had just started high school, so he wasn't around for Andy to turn to for a safe, familiar face. By this point, my husband was busy working on boats in beautiful Sydney Harbour, and I was working full-time, so there was no one home during the day.

My husband's work was flexible—after all, boats don't care what time you start—so he would drop both boys off at school in the morning. But sometimes, Andy would sneak out right after being dropped off, following Dad out of the school gates without anyone noticing. On other days, he'd leave the school during school hours. This caused quite a stir, as the school was responsible for his safety during school hours.

I had no idea what anxiety really looked like. I would have imagined a child appearing timid, scared, and crying, but Andy was cool, calm, and clearly had a plan. He just couldn't communicate his feelings, which left me frazzled and upset over his behavior. One day, I got a call from the school saying they had contacted the police, and I had to rush home to see if Andy was there. I remember crying as I drove along the freeway, completely unsure of what to do.

Then I recalled that one of my sister's close friends was a social worker. She was super cool and funky, and I thought Andy would feel comfortable talking to her. So, while I was on my way home, I decided to give her a call.

At first, she was hesitant to get involved since we knew each other socially, and she warned me that things might get awkward if there were uncomfortable truths about my parenting. But I was desperate. "I don't care, Rachel! I have no shame. I'm not the perfect mum, and I'll be the first to admit it. I'll do whatever it takes to help him.

Please help us!"

Social Work

What it is

The international federation of social workers describes Social Work as "a practice-based profession and an academic discipline that promotes social change and development, social cohesion, and the empowerment and liberation of people. Principles of social justice, human rights, collective responsibility and respect for diversities are central to social work."

How it works

When Andy met with Rachel, it was a similar process to counselling. She spent the sessions talking with Andy to understand him and identify what sorts of approaches and tools could be useful to apply in his life both at home and at school. Rachel provided her observations and recommendations to the school for managing his Houdini acts, being the first person to identify that this was a display of anxiety – not disobedience.

Our experience

Rachel was amazing at connecting with Andy. She had this relaxed vibe that made it easy for them to chat. I loved how she used picture cards for him to select his responses. The emotions represented on those cards helped him express himself in ways he hadn't been able to before. She'd ask him a question, and he'd pick a card that reflected his answer. It was a real game-changer for me, and that's when I had a lightbulb moment. Suddenly, I understood Andy on a whole new level, and I realized just how misunderstood he had been all his life—by me, by teachers, by kids, by everyone!

After spending some time alone with Andy, we'd all come together as a family to chat with Rachel. She uncovered that the real issue wasn't the classroom itself but the overwhelming chaos of the playground. School felt tough for him, while home was his safe haven. Rachel proposed some strategies for the school to help manage his Houdini acts and create a more supportive environment.

She found Andy to be insightful, creative, and honest. He was respectful of her approach and engaged with her much more easily than most kids his age, showing his intelligence. Rachel suggested that he wasn't being oppositional just for the sake of it; he was getting overwhelmed and didn't know how to cope with those feelings. This, combined with a lack of impulse control, led to the behaviors we were witnessing.

She recommended that we see a psychiatrist, as she suspected that Andy might have Asperger's (now known as Autism Level 1) and possibly other neurological issues.

Psychiatry

What it is

Psychology Today describes Psychiatry as a "specialty of medicine that focuses on researching, understanding, diagnosing, and treating diseases of the brain and disorders of the mind and behavior. Psychiatrists diagnose and treat a wide range of conditions, from Alzheimer's disease, anxiety, and autism to mood disorders, psychosis, and suicidality." If you ask me, the description is simple: psychiatrists prescribe medications.

How it works

A psychiatrist will gather as much information about the patient as possible, by talking to teachers, parents and the patient themselves. Following the initial assessment and diagnosis, psychiatrists will spend sessions talking to their patient to determine how the medication is working and if any adjustments are required (or, if no medication is being taken, if it is required).

The way I think about the difference between psychologists and psychiatrists is the ability to prescribe medicines. Psychiatrists have a prescription pad and psychologists do not. Often following a diagnosis, the prescription pad comes out.

Our experience

Our psychiatrist recommended a Clinical Psychologist to assess Andy, who conducted a couple of tests and confirmed that Andy had:

- Attention Deficit Hyperactivity Disorder (ADHD)
- Anxiety
- Level 1 Autism
- Oppositional Defiance Disorder (ODD)

However, the clinical psychologist believed that once we managed Andy's ADHD and Autism effectively, the ODD wouldn't be as apparent—and he was right.

When you're caring for a child with multiple needs, you don't just jump straight into medicating everything. It's all about a slow and steady approach, allowing us to assess, adjust, and stabilize the effects of each medication before moving on to the next issue in line.

We agreed that anxiety was Andy's most pressing concern, so he was prescribed Fluoxetine. This medication made a noticeable difference in his difficult behavior and those Houdini acts of his. Before long, we started trialing him on short-acting Ritalin for ADHD, and it was a real game-changer. Andy began coping much better with day-to-day challenges.

I know there's a lot of concern around medicating children for ADHD, and I had my reservations too. But by the time we finally got around to diagnosing Andy, we were feeling pretty desperate, and the medication turned out to be really helpful.

It became clear to me that Andy wasn't waking up each day thinking, "I'm going to be naughty and difficult today." He was waking up wondering how he was going to manage another day. The medications helped him, and he was thrilled to be doing better at school. We were relieved to have a more relaxed and easier-going child, and the teachers were happy too, enjoying a more compliant and easier-to-teach Andy. At this stage, I'm definitely pro-meds!

2019 in summary

2019 was a pivotal year so I'm going to recap the key activities so you can appreciate how much time and effort these things take. It's a long and expensive process.

- We started January with the primer pyrrole tablets taking effect and helping calm him slightly.
- In March we reach out to Rachel to help us, and we continued to have sessions with her up until August, when the psychiatrist took over.
- We commence with the psychiatrist in July. She recommends an assessment.
- Throughout July and August, we continue our sessions with the clinical psychologist, and have regular sessions that will continue for several years with the psychiatrist.
- By September we have a diagnosis and have commenced trialling medication. With the diagnosis, school can now apply for additional support they need to help him in the classroom.
- We finish the year with a diagnosis, medications for both anxiety and ADHD and a pretty good outlook for 2020.

Chapter 6

Year 5 and the Diagnosis Journey

Now that we had a diagnosis, things started moving in the right direction. The school was extremely grateful and noticed significant improvements in how they could manage Andy in the classroom.

Diagnosis is far more than just a label—it brings some important benefits, like funding for the school, access to medication, and a deeper understanding of what's going on. For me, the biggest perk was finally having something to Google! I had never really known anyone with autism, and my knowledge of it was pretty limited and outdated.

I stumbled upon a YouTube channel called "Aspergers From The Inside," where Paul, who has autism himself, shares insightful and interesting weekly videos on various topics related to autism. Watching these videos gave me a new appreciation for the reality that Andy was living in. Some of the key insights I learned from Paul were:

- The sensory implications of being in crowded places like shopping malls and how this can be overwhelming.
- Emotions are displayed differently, and while they may look like they have no emotions, it is just that they are not being displayed.
- The constant effort it takes to fit in and anxiety of social situations, always being anxious to say the right things and afraid of missing the subtle complexities in communications, resulting in getting tired and crashing when you get home. No wonder Andy tanks in the afternoons!
- That "high functioning" autism is NOT what you think it is:
  - It has nothing to do with functioning. It was coined to refer to someone with autism who has above average IQ

- High functioning actually means *invisible struggle*. It does **not** mean reduced level of difficulty. Whatever struggles they are going through, are not visible to others. They are appearing to be doing well. But the amount of effort it takes to do really well takes them to their limit. This is why kids suddenly crash or meltdown. It becomes too much. Therefore, high functioning means working really hard behind the scenes to appear functioning. The stress is always there.
  - The biggest challenge is that other people don't understand because they don't see the internal struggle that costs a lot of energy behind the scenes.
- Wrong Planet Syndrome
  - It feels like a lot of the time, that they are not of the same species to the people around them. They see other people all doing the same thing and they somehow have a connection and know what to do, and that leaves them to wonder "what did I miss"?
  - It's like being transported into a foreign culture "why is everyone offended by this thing that I just did?"
  - A lot of people on the spectrum are extremely good cross-culturally, because they grow up with no culture (they feel like a foreigner in their own culture). It is easier when they are in another culture because they have an excuse not to understand while it is expected of them in their own culture.

- Burnout and anxiety are common
  - As you can see from the above points, burnout is common and when you feel burnt out, you need to take the time to recover.

If you know someone with autism, I highly recommend following Aspergers From the Inside on YouTube. Paul has helped me to better understand and therefore support Andy.

The assessment report came with a long list of recommendations for actions we could take to help Andy, with one of the top recommendations being to find a Speech Pathologist. I had always thought that Speech Therapy was for people who had issues such as a lisp so I was very intrigued by what Andy would get out of this.

Speech Therapy

What is it

Allied Health Professions Australia describes Speech Pathologists as those who "study, diagnose and treat communication disorders, including difficulties with speaking, listening, understanding language, reading, writing, social skills, stuttering and using voice. They work with people who have difficulty communicating because of developmental delays, stroke, brain injuries, learning disability, intellectual disability, cerebral palsy, dementia and hearing loss, as well as other problems that can affect speech and language."

How it works

Olivia helped Andy with his difficulty understanding others and sharing his thoughts, ideas and feelings appropriately. She used plenty of visuals and worksheets to navigate through the learning process. She also provided and developed strategies to help him through specific situations.

Our experience

Andy met with Olivia every fortnight, and we found those sessions incredibly helpful. She guided Andy in processing situations he was facing at school, helping him analyze, understand, and develop a new, deeper perspective on his behavior and actions.

Olivia also ran through play scenarios where a kid might do something, and they would discuss how Andy would react and feel in that situation. Because Andy needed to consciously learn and process these concepts that most of us pick up instinctively, he developed a depth of understanding and wisdom that's not typical for someone his age.

We're All a Bit on the Spectrum

Whenever I shared with friends that Andy had been diagnosed with autism, a common response was, "Oh, we're all a little bit on the spectrum." While I understand the intention behind that statement, please, don't say it. It feels invalidating. Now, when someone makes that comment, I respond with "Please tell me, how does your autism impact your ability to function?"

Year 5

In 2020 things felt stable for us. We spent a lot of weekends enjoying bush walks, and Andy developed a great friendship, which remains to this day. Andy has always been more comfortable with one or two close friends rather than large groups. His friend shares a similar disposition, and together, they happily blend board games with computer games and take walks with the dog. Neither of them feels at ease in a big group, and they don't feel the pressure to be cool or fit in with others. They're just being themselves—take it or leave it!

Our normal

At home, life continued in our own version of normal. Andy maintained his fascination with horror, devouring every Goosebumps book by R.L. Stine, and he enjoyed drawing pictures filled with death, blood, and gore. He also developed an odd fascination with smoke at a young age, which came with his impulse control issues. One memorable story stands out: our next-door neighbor, a smoker, often lit up outside by their garage. One day, while being homeschooled and with everyone else out of the house,

Andy snuck over, found the cigarettes, and brought them home. When my husband caught him in the act, he remembered hearing that a good way to deter a child from smoking was to make them smoke an entire pack, causing nausea. Andy took a slow, deliberate drag while staring down his dad, making it clear that strategy wasn't going to work. My husband quickly snatched the cigarette back. Oh, Andy.

What draws Andy to smoking is the way the tendrils of smoke curl and dance. So, I thought, easy fix! I'd buy him some incense sticks to watch the smoke. That didn't really cut it, though. For his birthday, we got him a fancy smoke machine, which was perfect— he could fill his whole room with smoke while dancing, complete with party lights and a disco ball. It was great for parties, but unfortunately, it still didn't fully satisfy his fascination with cigarettes. Bummer.

While neither of my boys were particularly sporty, we had a rule that they both had to choose one sport. Andy decided to follow in his older brother's footsteps, picking up baseball in the summer and AFL in the winter. He was okay at baseball—not the best, but not the worst either—so it was a good fit for him. AFL was a great way to get him out and about, but as the years went on, the other boys improved, and the games became more competitive. Andy began to find these games increasingly stressful. Coordination can be tough for kids with autism, and when primary school finished, so did his weekend sports.

A special shout-out goes to Andy's AFL coach, a local mum from school. She was brilliant with him, understanding and seeing the beautiful little guy he is. I ran into her recently, and she expressed how much she loved Andy. As a parent, hearing that about your child means the world, especially when so many people struggle to understand and tolerate him.

With the school environment becoming more stable and sports providing social opportunities, we still faced challenges. Andy was rarely invited to parties or social events, and that hasn't really changed. However, as his self-awareness grew, he began to understand that group situations weren't his strong suit. When one of the nicest boys in his class, whom Andy considered his best friend, didn't invite him to his birthday party, Andy wasn't upset. He realized he wouldn't have enjoyed it anyway, and he never held a grudge. Andy is the sweetest, most understanding, and caring friend anyone could wish for.

In contrast, Liam, with his easy-going nature, was well-liked by classmates, parents, and teachers, making school social events enjoyable for him. However, both my husband and I never felt entirely comfortable at social events for Andy's class, regardless of the school. I have a few friends with kids like Andy, and I know it's not just us who feel this way. There's something about being the parent of a "naughty" or "different" child that can leave you feeling a bit isolated socially. While it's not a major concern for me—I know who my friends are and love them dearly—it's important to acknowledge that this can be a tough situation for many parents, as school events can often be uncomfortable for them too.

I remember at Andy's Year 6 farewell, I found myself reluctant to socialize with the parents who had responded to playdate requests with a blunt "we're busy." I certainly didn't want to mingle with the parents of the kids who had bullied Andy relentlessly. Instead, we ended up chatting most of the evening with a lovely couple who had a beautiful girl that Andy had been in preschool with—she had missed a lot of school due to health issues.

Sleep issues

Did I mention earlier that Andy wasn't much of a sleeper? Sleep was always a challenge from the moment he encountered horror. As a hypnotherapist and someone who meditates regularly, I had a few tools at my disposal that I tried to put to good use.

Here's a typical evening: I'd invest a good chunk of my time gently inducing Andy into a sleepy, hypnotic state. After about 20-30 minutes of careful, soothing meditative induction, I'd quietly back out of the room, feeling hopeful. But just as I'd think I was finally off the hook, I'd hear him call out, "Mum!" as I walked down the hall. "I'm not tired."

Talk about frustrating! All I wanted was a normal evening to sit down, watch TV, and unwind after the kids went to bed. I'm not proud to admit it, but I would get angry with him.

"For fuck's sake Andy, just go to sleep!"

"But I can't. I'm not tired."

"It's easy. Close your eyes."

"I'm not tired."

Sigh.

The meditation sprinkled with hypnotic suggestions of sleepiness would work occasionally—usually the first time I tried that approach. It was like a one-hit wonder; if I tried the same technique again, it simply wouldn't work. Darn! I began to feel resentful, wishing I had a 'normal' child so I could enjoy normal evenings.

It was also common to wake up in the middle of the night to the sound of footsteps and quiet breathing next to my head. Andy would come stand beside me at whatever-o'clock until I finally stirred (I'm a light sleeper, so it didn't take long). I'd pull him into bed with me, and more often than not, he'd fall asleep between me and my husband. That was a good night.

At first, we were hesitant to give him sleeping medication, but eventually, melatonin became a nightly staple. It helped a bit, but it was never a guaranteed fix. Most nights, Andy would sneak downstairs to raid the fridge, watch movies, and light candles (yes, play with fire—yikes! And yes, I threw away everything that could start a fire, but somehow lighters always found their way back home). Oh, Andy. Keeping tabs on him was nearly impossible, so we ended up stacking two mattresses on top of each other next to our king-size bed. Our room looked like it had one super-de-dooper long bed!

I tried to keep a diary a few times, but I never managed to stick with it. Recently, I stumbled upon a note I took after one of those typical (maybe once-a-week) nights:

- Got bullied at school
- Was off mentally all afternoon, and is being weird
- Didn't want to sleep
- Gave melatonin and a Phenergan at 7.30pm
- He was tired at 9.30pm but restless so I gave him a massage for a while
- Attitude changed for the worse and wants to see the dog
- At 10pm gave another Phenergan
- He is reading in bed and won't get under the sheets (clearly indicating his intention to get up as soon I leave the room)
- His tummy is funny, he has eaten a chocolate bar he bought from the shops with $50 he stole from his dad's wallet
- Still reading at 10.30pm
- Got up and let him watch cartoons
- 2am got him to attempt sleep again and he went to bed

I started reading him children's classics like Haroun and the Sea of Stories, The Phantom Tollbooth, and anything by C.S. Lewis. We read and read and read. The moment I accepted and embraced this as my life, I found myself loving it. No more resentment! These became some of my fondest memories. It was such a joy having my husband, Andy, and me all lined up in our extra-long bed, reading and chatting. I felt like I should invite Liam in to join us! But no worries about FOMO—he was perfectly happy in his own room.

Sometimes Andy would drift off while I was reading; other nights were a bit more challenging. For those, we had Harry Nilsson's album, The Point. There's something so soothing about that story and the groovy '70s songs that often lulled Andy to sleep.

EMBRACE

Occasionally, he'd listen to the whole album, and then we'd switch to another favorite, Blue Dream, by Fiona Joy Hawkins. That album is absolutely beautiful—kudos to a musician who can create something you can listen to hundreds of times without getting tired of it!

At some point in 2020, Andy's sleep took a turn for the worse. While settling down was usually a pleasant experience (side note: sometimes he'd pretend to be asleep, or both his dad and I would nod off before he did), he'd soon be awake again and quietly sneak downstairs, inevitably up to some sort of mischief.

We went through a phase where he wouldn't sleep ALL NIGHT! I'd send him off to school the next day, bracing myself for a mess, but he'd come home bright-eyed and bushy-tailed. The silver lining of those all-nighters? He was sure to sleep through the following night. When he pulled an all-nighter, I tried to stay up with him to supervise (you might have realized by now that he's not the kind of kid you can leave unsupervised). I'd let him watch cartoons while I dozed on the couch. This exhausting cycle lasted a couple of months before I reached my breaking point. I couldn't cope anymore, so I asked the psychiatrist what she could do to help.

Andy was prescribed Clonidine, a medication typically used for blood pressure but with the lovely side effect of making you sleepy. It helped restore my sanity! While the Clonidine worked, he still had trouble staying asleep, so the psychiatrist kindly prescribed Quetiapine, an anti-psychotic drug—just half a tablet would knock him out all night.

As you can see, it took quite a cocktail of meds for Andy to achieve a full night of sleep. My poor baby. It took me a bit longer to adjust; I developed a habit of waking up at any little noise or randomly checking on him several times during the night to make sure he was still in bed.

The downside to all this sleep assistance was that he became terribly drowsy and difficult to wake up in the morning.

Update: I'm now able to sleep soundly all night! I no longer worry about Andy, as he's well into his teens and has matured enough that if he can't sleep, he can make himself a warm milk, grab a snack, watch a bit of TV, and take himself back to bed when needed. Occasionally, he might take a melatonin, but he's no longer on any pharmaceutical sleep aids.

Andy slept in our room for about 7 years, and I loved it. Not only was it a beautiful bonding experience, but my inner "helicopter parent" was also quite satisfied. I always knew the day would come when he'd want to sleep in his own room, and I dreaded that day. When it finally came, he moved into his own room, and thanks to all the sleep support he was on at the time, it went smoothly— especially after we bought him a big, comfy double bed!

My beautiful, caring boy

Every December, we celebrate an early Christmas with our Sydney-based cousins. My boys are the eldest, followed by eight younger children, ranging in age from 12 down to toddlers, including a set of twins. One of the twins was unusually quiet and clung tightly to his mum. When they arrived, Andy went out to greet them. He took one look at the little boy and said,

"Hello, you're like me – come with me."

Andy reached in to help him out of his car seat, and to everyone's surprise, especially his mum's, the little boy held out his arms to Andy without hesitation—something he never did with anyone else!

For the rest of the day, the boy stayed glued to Andy, holding his hand the entire time. Andy was gentle, kind, and took care of him with such tenderness. It was truly a beautiful thing to witness.

The name change

You might have noticed in Andy's earlier drawing that he called himself Aiden. He was born Aiden Jurkowski. Before his birth, my husband and I had considered naming him Andy, but somewhere during the pregnancy, we changed our minds and settled on Aiden. After his diagnosis, we shared this backstory with him, and he decided his days as Aiden were behind him. He felt new and improved and wanted to be called Andy.

It must be challenging to suddenly call someone by a different name after knowing them as Aiden their entire life. But our family fully supported his choice at home, and it quickly became normal for us. School, however, was a different story. It took a long time for the name change to be accepted, and there seemed to be resistance from the teachers. I was even told they couldn't call him Andy because he was registered in the system as Aiden. I didn't buy that for a second—are they telling me they've never referred to someone by a nickname?

Regardless, I backed Andy 100%, and we formally changed his name through the registry of births, deaths, and marriages, getting him a new birth certificate as Andy. He would often come home with A.N.D.Y written across his knuckles, and if anyone called him Aiden, he would cheekily flash his fist toward them, making sure they remembered his new name.

Chapter 7

Year 6 & Post Diagnosis Struggles

As we entered 2020, the world watched in fear as chaotic scenes unfolded in China, struggling to cope with a new and terrible virus: COVID. I remember being at the gym in early January when the entire room stopped exercising, fixated on the news screen covering the unfolding crisis with a sense of dread. It wasn't long before we were all working from home, plunged into full lockdown. It was such an eerie and unforgettable time.

The COVID lockdown was a difficult period for many people, but Andy was not one of them. I kept him home for the first few weeks, but since the school remained open for parents who couldn't work remotely, I eventually began sending him back so I could focus on my job. For the first time in a long while—possibly ever—Andy had no issues attending school. It was perfect for him. The quiet, calm environment during lockdown felt like a reprieve.

His speech therapist, who had moved to France and recently had a baby, decided to stop holding sessions to become a full-time mum. With lockdown in place, it didn't really matter if she was in Sydney or halfway across the world since the sessions would have been on Zoom anyway. We decided to take a break from speech therapy until Andy returned to more regular social interactions.

During the first few weeks of lockdown, while Andy was still doing his schooling from home, he had been playing the drums, sometimes accompanied by some bold, Marilyn Manson-style makeup. Although he wiped most of it off, there was still some left around his eyes when he appeared on a Zoom call, and, as you can imagine, it became a prime target for bullies. They had found their mark, and it followed him for the rest of the year.

The latter half of the year was hell for Andy as restrictions were lifted and kids returned to school from lockdown. Being bullied is never easy, but it escalated to the point where he began to self-harm. On days when he couldn't bear to face school, I would let him stay home, and we would spend 'mental health days' together.

School was never a happy place for Andy, and he was incredibly relieved when his primary school days came to an end. Fortunately, all the bullies were headed to a private school, while the kinder kids were going to the same local high school as Andy. Thank God!

It wasn't until over a year later, when Andy's depression became severe, that he opened up about what had really happened at school. He called Lifeline and revealed to the person on the phone that a teacher had bullied him. She humiliated him in front of the class, showing no compassion or kindness. I was devastated to hear this so long after the fact, wishing I had known earlier so I could have stood up for him. I strongly believe teachers need better education and tools to manage children with neurological disorders, not to belittle them in front of their peers.

Andy told me how she would single him out in front of the other students, loudly reprimanding him and embarrassing him. It was clear this treatment gave a green light to the bullies, because in Andy's eyes, she was just another bully. She made him sit alone at the front of the class, never allowing him to share a desk like the other kids, further isolating him. When he asked for help with the bullying, she did nothing.

I empathize with teachers—it's no easy job, and except for this one teacher, most have been wonderful to Andy. It doesn't take much to see that Andy isn't a 'bad kid.' Despite his challenges, he has never hurt anyone unless provoked and has never acted cruelly. His behaviors have always been self-destructive or destructive to property—never toward others. The way this teacher treated him left a deep scar, one that we've continued to work through for years.

For the love of music

Andy was a brilliant dancer, and music had been his passion since he was a toddler. When he was little, he adored Michael Jackson and would dance for hours, completely lost in the rhythm. Andy had music in his soul—when he danced, people couldn't help but stop and watch. He was truly remarkable. One long weekend we went to a farm party on the NSW mid-north coast called the 'Longview Farm Party.' They featured a classic Aussie band on Saturday night, with smaller bands playing throughout the weekend. Andy always found himself on the dancefloor when the band played, and they loved him and he attracted quite a bit of attention! When he danced, it was just him, the music, and the moment.

He later started drum lessons and quickly mastered them, spending countless hours banging away on the drums. Though he was never a sporty kid, playing the drums gave him an intense, full-body workout as his arms energetically and forcefully struck the drums and feet worked furiously with the foot pedals. Not long after, he began learning the electric and bass guitar. Andy became obsessed with Rage Against the Machine, which I didn't mind at all since I loved them back in the '90s.

At some point, his musical taste took a darker turn, and he got into heavy metal, followed by death metal. Oh no. He went through so many phases with different music genres, and I hoped the death metal phase would pass quickly. He was drawn to the technicality of the drumming, and it helped him release some of his teenage angst. It took a couple of years for him to move on from death metal, although he still listens to it from time to time.

Now, he's completely hooked on Korn. For a long time, they were the only band he listened to, and I have to admit, I've grown to love them too. I understand why Andy is so obsessed with them. Jonathan Davis's raw, emotional singing is something Andy deeply connects with. Listening to, playing, and singing along to Korn has become his form of daily therapy.

While we had a couple of relatively stable years with his medication, there was still room for improvement. I began looking for another speech therapist, but COVID had made it nearly impossible to find one. It seemed like the pandemic had affected all the kids, and therapists were in high demand.

During my search for a speech or occupational therapist, I stumbled across a therapy called Tomatis. It was expensive, but it sounded promising, and we were all in.

Tomatis

What it is

Named after Dr Alfred Tomatis, who developed the method in the early 1950's, the Tomatis Method is a neurosensory program that utilizes music (mostly by Mozart) to retrain the auditory processing, balance, and coordination or connections between the ear, brain, and body.

The ear, a "sensory gate," serves as an access to the brain to create change. The Tomatis® Method generally:

- Improves attention, concentration, focus, and memory
- Develops language, speech, communication and socialisation
- Enhances learning skills like reading and comprehension
- Boosts self-awareness and confidence
- Reduces anxiety and stress
- Promotes better quality of life (such as sleep and appetite)

Source: tomatis.com.au

How it works

The method involves listening to music played over a special headphone and player. The modified or filtered music stimulates parts of the ear responsible for transmitting information to the brain. This auditory stimulation retrains the brain and re-patterns the nervous system, which leads to improvement in physical, cognitive, and interpersonal skills and emotional regulation.

Sound healing directs specific sounds, creating vibrations that impact a person's well-being. The "Mozart Effect" is one of the most famous sound therapies. A study suggests listening to Mozart's music for 10 minutes enhances a person's spatial-temporal reasoning performance. Some claim that other than cognitive performance, it influences emotions, too.

Music healing uses music to communicate for people who have difficulty expressing their feelings and thoughts in words. It is a way of eliciting engagement or active participation of a person by creating music, which leads to positive health results.

Sound training promotes music as stimulation to identify and create frequencies specific to the listener.

Our experience

The baseline hearing test showed a marked difference between the left and right ears, indicating issues with how his brain processes auditory information. The initial test also showed that in some cases he hears more predominantly with bone conduction over air hearing. I'm not exactly sure what that means, however, the aim of the program was to get Andy's hearing to a 'normal' looking graph.

Andy and I both got headsets, and it was required for both of us to listen to the music together. We did this daily for up to 40 minutes, twice a day. It was a nice opportunity to relax and enjoy Mozart or other soothing music.

We did notice results—Andy became more grounded, calm, and cooperative. The effects were subtle, much like what we had experienced with LENS therapy. What was particularly curious, though, was that Andy developed phobias of spiders and needles. These phobias lasted for about 12 months, during which time it was impossible to draw blood from him, as he would completely panic at the sight of a needle or a spider.

By the time we completed the *very expensive* Tomatis program, Andy had developed two phobia's, was a bit easier with basic tasks at home, and seemed more grounded and centered.

The Tomatis program wasn't the magic wand we had desperately hoped for. Toward the end of the program, during the school holidays, we took a quick trip to visit an old friend of mine who lived a few hours up the coast. She had two daughters, one close in age to Andy. I thought it would be perfect—they could hang out while I caught up with my dear friend.

It turned out to be a disaster.

Her daughter had a friend over, and neither of them liked Andy. He didn't fit in, and they made it clear they didn't want him around. My poor boy ended up either watching TV or sticking close to me and my friend. I had forgotten to pack the Tomatis headphones, which gave us a good excuse to cut the visit short and head home early.

MARNIE JURKOWSKI

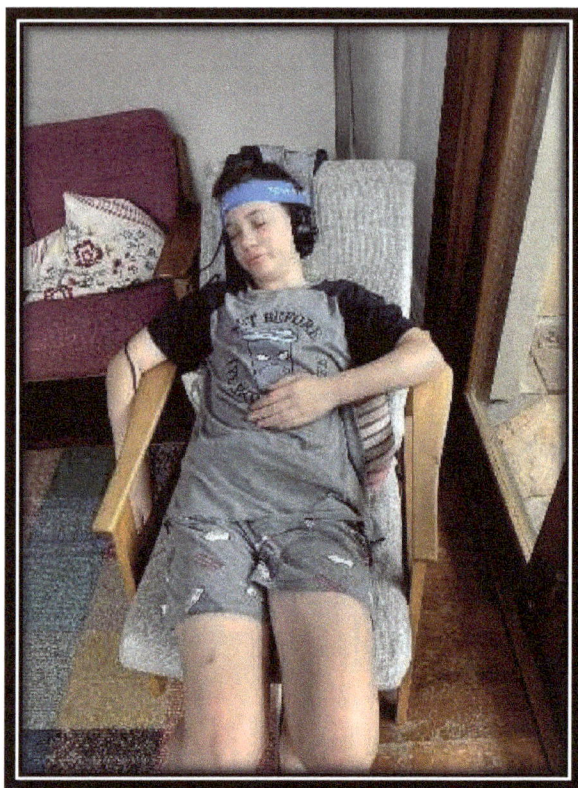

Andy listening to Mozart on the Tomatis headphones

Chapter 8

High School Years

13 – 15 years old

I was incredibly nervous about Andy starting high school and how he would cope. He's easily influenced, and I feared that if he fell in with the wrong crowd, it could take our situation from bad to worse. I had an appointment with a psychic I had been waiting 18 months to see—she's highly sought after, which is why the wait was so long. The timing of the session was perfect, coming just before Andy was about to begin high school. She gave me the reassurance I desperately needed.

"It's not going to be smooth sailing, it will have its challenges, but it will be a better experience than primary school. There will be people at the school who really look out for him and have his back."

She was right.

Year 7

The start of high school went smoothly, and Andy even made a couple of nice new friends. The school was better equipped, with a learning support unit to help manage kids like him. He enjoyed his 30-minute walk to school, headphones on, listening to his music. The first term seemed to be going well—until the final week, when he was given a short suspension for "aggressive behavior."

As usual, Andy's bully beacon had been sending out those familiar "tease me" vibes, and before long, he was being regularly harassed.

I know Andy doesn't help himself, ever since he had been watching horror, he had become the weird kid and would say things that weren't appropriate. He's the one who takes things too far. For example – if a bunch of kids are talking about farting and giggling and joking around, Andy will be the one to take it to the next level (too far) and end up making everyone uncomfortable.

Following the short suspension, I had a discussion with the school, arguing that Andy was being punished for being the one to crack under constant harassment. Their response: "We treat everyone the same. Rules are rules. We cannot tolerate violence. He simply cannot react with violence."

Fine.

We accepted the suspension, and within days of his return, during a physical education class on the basketball court, the same kid who had pushed him into aggressive behavior and caused his suspension struck again—this time running up behind Andy and pulling down his shorts, 'dacking' him.

Andy took a deep breath, counted to ten, and told the teacher. He didn't get in trouble because he managed to control his reaction. I was so proud of him. Not reacting in that kind of situation is hard for anyone, but for Andy, with all his emotional regulation difficulties, it was a huge achievement. The next time I saw the teacher who had suspended him, I said, "Do you understand what I meant earlier? Can you see now that he gets in trouble because he's bullied, and he snaps. Now you see it, too. Welcome to Andy's world."

It wasn't long before Andy was suspended again, and this time, I was really upset. I understand the need for consequences, but this was ridiculous. Andy was being bullied, had repeatedly asked teachers for help, and had begged the bully to stop. With no support from the teacher and pushed to his limit, he lashed out, pushing the boy's head into a desk. Andy was suspended once more. We were told the teacher had planned to deal with the situation after class. How was Andy supposed to know that?

This time, he got two weeks off school. He was sent to a small 'suspension center' at a local primary school, set up specifically for kids who had been suspended. It accommodated only two or three students, and the two teachers there were specially trained to work with kids like Andy. The schedule was shorter, starting late and finishing early, and he received one-on-one attention for most of the day. He loved it. This was Andy's dream school.

He even met another sweet and sensitive boy at the suspension center who was just like him. Later on, they'd meet again at an independent high school set up to support young people who don't cope with mainstream school. I think this perfectly illustrates my point: our beautiful, sensitive children are punished simply because they can't cope. Surely, our school and mental health systems can do better, right?

❤ ❤ ❤ ❤

I want to take a moment to talk about the different levels of Autism, which reflect the amount of support required for daily functioning. There are three levels:

- **ASD Level 1: Requiring Support** – Individuals may struggle with communication, particularly with neurotypical peers.

- **ASD Level 2: Requiring Substantial Support** – They may find it difficult to communicate in socially acceptable ways.

- **ASD Level 3: Requiring Very Substantial Support** – Individuals may be unable to mask their behaviors and face significant challenges with self-regulation.

Source: Understanding the Three Levels of Autism by Lisa Jo Judy. Verywell health Jan 09, 2024

I often wonder if having ASD Level 1 is worse because you appear "normal" and seem capable of functioning like everyone else. You attend the same institutions as "typical" people, which leads others to impose the same expectations on you that they have for everyone else.

This results in unrealistic demands placed on our already stressed-out kids, who are at breaking point just trying to navigate their daily lives, let alone keep up. When they fail to meet these impossible standards, they face punishment, and it truly breaks my heart. It really does.

♥ ♥ ♥ ♥

As you can see, I'm no stranger to receiving calls from schools requesting meetings. These encounters are never enjoyable, and we've been summoned to countless meetings at every school Andy has attended. I never quite get used to them, and they always bring a familiar sense of dread to the pit of my stomach.

When you arrive at the school for one of these dreaded meetings, you're usually shown into a room with a round table where a head teacher, the principal, the learning support teacher, and the school counsellor sit. There's always a box of tissues on hand. They proceed to inform you of concerning behaviors, and it's around this time that tears well up and a lump forms in my throat. I start to feel like a failure. Why can't I manage my son? Why does he exhibit these behaviors? Over time, the emotions tied to these meetings evolve. Instead of guilt and shame, I now feel a profound sadness about the unfairness of the situation and the consequences for Andy, which often culminate in a suspension.

Suspension is intended to serve as a punishment for the child who misbehaves. It's already challenging enough parenting a child with additional needs, and having to navigate them through a prolonged suspension only adds to the difficulty. So, who is really being punished here?

Meanwhile, we had arranged for Liam to participate in a six-month international student exchange program in the Netherlands, so we took a short family holiday in Fiji before sending our firstborn across the globe.

As with all vacations, Andy was fantastic—we relaxed and enjoyed our time together. He joined us for kayaking, swimming, and snorkeling. However, being 13, he found himself in a bit of a no-man's land at the resort. There was a kiddie pool filled with squealing toddlers, and an adults-only pool where he wasn't allowed to hang out. This is something to consider when planning a holiday at a resort island with teenagers.

In November, after being on a waiting list, a spot opened up with a psychologist, and Andy began seeing the clinical psychologist who had originally assessed him and confirmed his diagnosis back in 2019.

Psychologist

What it is

A psychologist is someone who uses talk therapy to help someone process their thoughts and emotions.

How it works

A psychologist session involves talking about what you want help with and helping the psychologist to understand your difficulties. The psychologist will ask questions to make sure they understand as much as possible. Following this, they will help you develop a plan and use strategies and techniques to overcome the issues you are experiencing.

Our experience

In Andy's case, he would often say very little in a session, resulting in us spending a reasonable sum of money for very little outcome.

There is an expectation that, as a parent, you are providing your child with everything you can to support them. Agree wholeheartedly. However, part of this expectation is that, of course, your child is seeing a psychologist at a minimum.

In our experience we were not getting much value for money. Again, I want to caution you that this is our experience and I believe it is a very necessary support for many people. It is just that sitting on a couch and talking wasn't going to be what was going to help Andy. Kids need to unload their issues otherwise, the psychologist has nothing to work with. Andy wasn't giving him very much to work with. He also recommended that we allow Andy to watch TV and do his gaming as his escape and wind down.

Chapter 9

Mental Health Struggles

Year 8

The school staff were doing everything they could, but Andy was starting to pull off some Houdini-like disappearing acts—either not showing up for class or spending time in the sick bay. I was receiving multiple calls from the school each week, asking me to come and collect him from there.

Certain areas of the school triggered panic for Andy. For instance, there was a classroom he absolutely refused to enter and a hallway he wouldn't walk through.

One day, a teacher discovered him in a stairwell, engaging in self-harm. When he was taken to the school counsellor, Andy confided that he had a plan to commit suicide.

Mental health emergency

When someone has a plan to commit suicide, it becomes a mental health emergency. It is treated like a medical issue, so we went to our GP, who advised us to go to the hospital emergency department. Andy's brother has epilepsy, so we are used to Emergency departments and the long wait times that go with it. I can't remember what time we got home that night, but it was quite late. So my advice is, if you find yourself needing to go to the hospital for a mental health or other health emergency, make sure you have a bottle of water, some snacks, a laptop, a book and a phone charger.

While we were at the hospital, Andy was seen by Child & Youth Mental Health Service (CYMS).

Child Youth Mental Health Service (CYMHS)

What it is

It is a free, NSW state government service providing specialist mental health assessment and intervention to children (under 18 years old, or still at school) with moderate to severe and complex mental health problems and their families.

How it works

CYMHS provides a multidisciplinary and family-focused approach, providing evidence-based treatment which may include individual, parent, family therapy and group programs, delivered through one of their community-based teams or inpatient unit.

Our experience

Andy opened up to the CYHMS representative. He spent a long time talking with her. After which, she took me aside to fill me in on her conversation with Andy. She advised me that he had been watching disturbing content on the dark web and this was causing him distress and disturbing thoughts, which he was subsequently unable to process.

How could this happen? Apparently, via links that take you to a live streaming 'room' where he saw the disturbing content. Shit!

She helped him install a suicide prevention app on his phone (yes, the phone has parental controls) and he made a suicide prevention plan with a list of resources and numbers to call.

We had a home visit within a couple of weeks and the CYHMS representatives were impressed with Andy's openness and willingness to be helped. This, along with a healthy home environment and considering the existing therapies and support in place, he was deemed as not requiring further CYHMS support.

They provided contact numbers, and a safety plan and left us to it.

We felt that they were making sure that we were able to provide the support and environment he needed and they were satisfied that his issues were not to do with abusive parenting.

Safety Plan

A safety plan is very simple, and it provides a list of things to do if you are feeling very depressed and considering suicide. Andy's plan looked like this:

1. Talk to parent
2. Call Kids Helpline
3. Call local mental health team
4. Call 000

♥ ♥ ♥ ♥

As you know, I do my best to keep a close watch on Andy, but it's impossible to supervise him 24/7, especially while I'm sleeping. No matter how close we kept him by our bed, he somehow managed to access harmful content.

I realize that not every child is like Andy, who presents unique challenges on many fronts. Still, the reality is that our kids aren't safe as long as we have smartphones and smart TVs. We tried hiding the remote controls, but over time, he either discovered their hiding spots or we simply forgot at the end of a long day.

The outcome of the mental health emergency was a doubling of Andy's Fluoxetine dosage, the medication he takes for anxiety. At his next psychologist appointment, we were advised to take him out of school for at least the remaining two weeks of the term. The stress of school was causing him to self-harm and feel suicidal. Maybe after a four-week break, he would be ready to return. Maybe.

Distance Education

Not long into the new term, we were called in for a discussion with the school. They needed to talk. Despite their best efforts, the mainstream school system was not working for Andy, and we needed to begin exploring alternative options.

During the meeting, they outlined the process we would follow to get Andy into a school that could better cater to his needs. The current school would complete an access request form, written by the learning and support team. This form details Andy's challenges on his worst days to prioritize him against other children undergoing the same process.

A panel meets once a term to review this information and determine the best available placement. These schools are known as Schools for Specific Purposes (SSPs), each with different specializations and teachers trained for specific needs. For instance, one school specialized in emotional disturbances (ED).

The school walked us through the SSPs within a reasonable distance from our home. After the meeting, I went home and conducted some research. While I can't recall exactly what we decided in terms of our priorities, we filled out all the necessary forms for the committee to determine which special education program had the capacity to take Andy.

We lived very close to a Giant Steps school, which catered to students with level 2 and 3 autism. While Andy could be categorized as level 2 due to the impact of autism on his quality of life, I knew he would have hated it there. The children had much greater needs than he did, so unfortunately, this wasn't a realistic option for us.

In the meantime, we applied for Andy to attend Sydney Distance Education, designed to support families in remote parts of Australia but also offering a base in Sydney for kids like Andy. It felt reminiscent of the COVID experience. This time, however, Andy was older and understood that it wasn't education he disliked—it was the school environment. He was motivated to participate in the classes from the comfort of home. The only interactions with other students came through a screen, providing a safe space that shielded him from bullying, which he didn't have to worry about there. To avoid putting him under stress, he was placed on a "Year 8 light" curriculum, which was a breeze for him.

He didn't require too much supervision, and since I was working from home post-COVID, it was easy for me to ensure he joined his online classes.

At this stage, it was clear that the puberty blues had escalated into full-blown depression. His energy levels were low, motivation was nonexistent, and he found it impossible to feel joy. He struggled to communicate and often had trouble holding his head up at the dinner table. The weight of his depression was unbearable, and gaming became an escape from the dark thoughts that plagued him. Now that he was at home with a light school load, he had plenty of time to game.

I found myself stuck between a rock and a hard place. I'm not a fan of gaming and prefer to limit my kids' screen time, but how could I say no? Should I tell him to stop gaming and endure the full pain of life that sometimes drove him to self-harm?

We did allow him more gaming time than I would have liked. At every opportunity, we took him for bushwalks to get him outside and into nature. Walking the dog became Andy's responsibility, ensuring he was outside daily.

We managed to break up his gaming time with music. He continued attending band practice a couple of times a week and became obsessed with Korn, listening to their music for hours.

Physical Challenge

No matter which professional we have taken Andy to see, consistent advice is to get involved in some form of physical activity. Andy's depression was extreme, and it took a huge effort to get Andy to engage in much physical activity. Getting him out of the house or involved in a group activity was impossible, so we purchased a mini trampoline (otherwise known as a rebounder). He could watch TV or listen to music while he jumped. We discovered that this is also a great form of exercise, with 10 minutes of jumping being equal to a 30-minute run! That is how we have managed to get some exercise into his day.

❤ ❤ ❤ ❤

Chapter 10

Searching for Solutions

A friend of mine told me about a school that had been created specifically for kids like Andy, who either struggle to cope or refuse to attend school. She mentioned they were taking applications and were having an open day. We registered to attend and off we went.

Wow.

We were impressed by the little school, with their small and supportive community of teachers and students. Andy had a good feeling and wanted to be a part of it. I love that Andy has always wanted to learn, it's the environment that he has always struggled so hard to cope with. They only catered for Years 9 & 10, and at this stage, Andy was in Year 8.

We filled in an application form anyway. They are so lovely there, that while he was not able to go full time until Year 9, they invited him to attend one day a week for the rest of the year so he could get familiar with and adjust to the school. Brilliant!

Independent High School

I'm going to add the school as an intervention, because it was created to help young people like Andy to attend school who can't cope for a variety of reasons in the mainstream system, and it is an important part of Andy's healing journey.

What it is

The school is an independent high school created to provide opportunities for young people to thrive in an alternative education setting which is tailored to them. They provide a positive, inclusive, safe and personalized learning environment.

How it works

Small class sizes and a supportive learning environment with a focus on well-being before education. The personalized learning plans remove the stress of having to keep up with everyone else.

Our experience

Andy is very happy at this school, and we love it! They deliver on their promise of being a supportive, small and caring community of teachers and students who understand young people like Andy. A safe, respectful environment is essential for our sensitive souls. Andy has thrived there.

The school has now expanded to Year 11 and 12, and Andy loves school so much that he would like to complete Year 12, which had never been an option before.

♥ ♥ ♥ ♥

My eldest son, Liam, has always had a passion for planes. One year, when he was about seven, all he wanted for Christmas was an Antonov 225 model airplane. When I found out there was an airshow scheduled in Newcastle that November—such a beautiful time of year with the weather warming up before it got too hot—I thought it would be the perfect weekend getaway for our family. I grew up near the RAAF base and have fond memories of watching airshows as a young girl.

I booked a charming beach house in Stockton for three nights, just across the road from a stunning, sandy beach where the planes would soon be flying overhead. The weather was perfect, with blue skies as far as the eye could see. On our first day, we enjoyed a lovely walk around Newcastle, catching a little ferry across the harbor from Stockton. As with most outings, we had to entice Andy to join us by promising ice cream. I was looking forward to finding a nice restaurant or café for an early dinner after our walk.

However, Andy's tolerance wore thin the longer we walked, and his mood began to plummet. "Okay, let's just go out for dinner and head home," I suggested.

"No, I don't want to be out. I just want a takeaway pizza and to go home."

"Alright, we'll order you a pizza, and Dad and I will have a quick dinner out and see you at home."

My husband and I exchanged concerned glances, realizing we couldn't leave Andy in such a depressed state unsupervised. So, we all opted for takeaway pizza and settled in to watch TV back at the house.

The next day, Liam had just gotten his license and drove up to join us for the airshow. It was another beautiful day, and the airshow was impressive. Andy, however, wasn't as impressed; he tolerated it at best. His depression continued to spiral downwards, and all he wanted was to be home, so we decided to leave a day early. It seemed like weekends away were no longer the relaxing breaks they used to be.

I can't help but wonder if Andy's current addiction to gaming is part of the problem. What initially helped distract him from disturbing thoughts now seems to trap him, making it difficult for him to be away from the Xbox. In trying to manage one issue, we've inadvertently created another. Sigh.

In 2013, the Gillard government introduced the National Disability Insurance Scheme (NDIS), established to provide funding for eligible individuals with disabilities to gain more time with family and friends, achieve greater independence, and access new skills, jobs, or volunteering opportunities in their community. When Andy received his diagnosis in 2019, it was suggested that we apply for NDIS funding. However, I had heard from several sources that the approval process was very challenging, and since we weren't struggling financially, I felt that the funding should go to Australians who needed it more than we did.

As Andy's challenges became more complex and severe, I decided it was time to apply for NDIS funding. In August 2023, our application was approved, granting us $14,000 over three years. What a fortune! My first thought was, "How are we going to spend all this money?"

A friend mentioned a trial at Sydney Uni for a treatment called rTMS. This treatment is currently available only for adults, but they were running a trial to see if it could reduce the 'symptoms' of autism for teens aged 14 to 18. After doing some research, I found it promising, so we began the process of getting Andy into the trial.

rTMS

What it is

Repetitive Transcranial magnetic stimulation (rTMS) refers to applying recurring TMS pulses to a specific brain region.

How it works

An electromagnetic coil is placed against the scalp of your head. The coil delivers pulses that stimulate nerve cells in the region of your brain involved in mood control and depression. It's thought to activate regions of the brain that have decreased activity during depression. The stimulation appears to affect how the brain is working, eases symptoms of depression and improves mood.

Our experience

Due to Liam having epilepsy, we had to jump through a few extra hoops to get into the program, plus it was going to take a lot of commitment for us to do.

I was feeling desperate and of course, I'd do whatever it took to help my boy. If it meant driving an hour a day for 20 consecutive days for a treatment that he had a 50% chance of being in a placebo group, so be it. I was prepared to do it.

We had so very nearly jumped through all the hoops, the last one being an MRI. Andy does love to headbang when he listens to his music and surprise, surprise, they picked up some inflammation in the cervical area, which they wanted cleared first. More hoops (sigh).

It was at this time that one afternoon, my husband and I were out walking the dog and took a different route than usual and wandered past a place called Brain Hub. Plastered on the wall was a list of conditions that they help. We noticed that ADD/ADHD, Anxiety and Autism were listed. Interesting. Just around the corner from home.

I gave them a call and after my initial call with them, we booked in for an assessment. When I explained that we were trying to get Andy into the rTMS trial, they said that what they did at Brain Hub was essentially the same but without the use of magnets. Fabulous! At least we won't have to worry about being in a placebo group and getting nothing….and that hour drive was going to be a 5-minute walk down the road. Let's go. Oh, and it's expensive too. Thank God we had NDIS funding.

Brain Hub

What it is

Brain Hub is a vestibular rehabilitation and brain-based therapy clinic. This is a new and exciting field. Like Tomatis, it works with the vestibular system, which includes the structures inside the inner ear and helps the body with balance and movement.

How it works

Brain Hub uses neuroplasticity to reprogram the wiring of the brain. It uses functional neurology (also referred to as chiropractic neurology) to evaluate and treat the central and peripheral nervous system.

Based on chiropractic foundations, they employ vagal nerve stimulation and many other tools to stimulate areas of the brain.

Our experience

We quickly used up all of our NDIS funding in 3 short months. It was put to good use and we saw fantastic results. However, there were too many things on our list to resolve, and within the funding that we had, we were only able to tackle two: impulse control and sleep.

Andy's impulse control has improved to the point it is no longer a problem. His sleep had improved, too, and we were able to take him off the medications for sleep. Winning!

Hitting the bottom

The doubled dose of Fluoxetine didn't seem to make any difference at all; getting Andy out of his depression felt impossible. I was growing increasingly desperate. He resisted our attempts to get him outside, and during the last few bush walks, we literally had to force him to join us by threatening to take away his gaming privileges.

EMBRACE

We live in Sydney, home to some amazing coastal walks. One day, we decided to visit Clifton Gardens in Mosman, located on the north side of Sydney along the harbor. It was a stunning day, with a crystal blue sky and sparkling clear water as we strolled along a beautiful bush track. Feeling invigorated by our gorgeous surroundings, I paused and said, "Wow, Andy, just take a deep breath and enjoy this amazing place."

"I hate it. I want to go home."

♥ ♥ ♥ ♥

Chapter 11

Early Attempts to Shine Light into the

Darkness

Christmas of 2023 was a big family affair. My family is very close, and my parents had rented a large home in Byron Bay for our reunion. However, Andy's depression cast a shadow over the festivities. It's incredibly challenging to enjoy the moment when your child is so deeply down; all he wanted was to go home. I started to suspect that he might have agoraphobia since he was reluctant to leave the house, but I wasn't entirely convinced.

To complicate matters, Andy began feeling unwell daily, often vomiting in the mornings after taking his medications. We pinpointed the culprit, and the Primer Pyrrole went straight in the bin. I can't say I was too sorry to see it go—it was expensive!

His crippling depression was affecting the entire family, and holidays felt off the table for now. I was desperate to help him, and my intuition told me we were close to a breakthrough. I just knew we were going to find something to heal him soon. I couldn't tell if it was intuition or desperation, but I can say this: giving up was not an option. So many times, I felt overwhelmed, drained of energy, and out of options, wanting to throw my hands up in despair. But within seconds, I knew that was NEVER going to happen because failure was not an option. We will keep going until you get better, Andy. I promise.

Side note: In Hollywood films, it always annoys me when the hero character makes a promise that "everything is going to be okay." Because in real life, shit happens, and only in Hollywood can a buff hero promise an outcome they can't control. Oh well, here I go... "I promise, Andy, that I'll never give up. Never. You will get better, my darling, and you will live a happy and fulfilling life. Amen."

EMBRACE

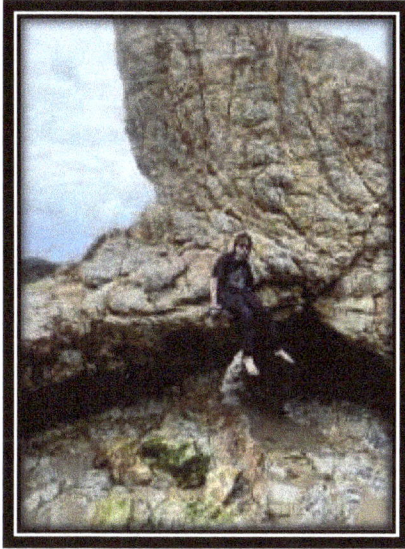

Andy trying to enjoy the family holiday.

Brain Hub has helped, but the progress is slow, and it's very expensive. Our NDIS funding has run out, so I applied for additional support. After a long four-month wait, I received an extra $9,000, but it came with restrictions: the funds could only be used for occupational therapy, speech therapy, and assisted daily living costs. They explicitly noted that additional funding for Brain Hub was declined.

That initial $14,000, which seemed like a fortune that I would struggle to spend, ended up covering very little. At least we managed to secure funding for 4 out of the 6 months of Brain Hub, and for that, I am genuinely grateful.

❤ ❤ ❤ ❤

Andy would often say things like, "I'm never going to get better" and he was in a constant negative state of mind.

I wanted to help him to reframe, as I do believe that we create our own reality through our beliefs. What do I mean by that? If I believe that everyone hates me and someone asks me to please move out of their way, I will interpret that as "I'm nobody, I'm not important, of course they want me out of their way."

However, if I am in a positive frame of mind and get asked to please move, I will not take it personally and realize that they are not thinking about me, and it is not a reflection on my worthiness as a human being.

I often listen to a wonderful podcast called "Feel Better, Live More" by Dr Rangan Chatterjee. While walking the dog one morning, I listened to episode #413, How to Make 2024 Your Best Year: 3 Questions to Ask Yourself Each Day.

In this episode, Dr Chatterjee recommends you ask yourself 3 questions every morning and 3 questions each evening. I started using the morning questions with my family the moment I got home!

Journalling

What it is

Journalling requires you to take a moment out of your day to reflect and write. Dr Chatterjee suggests that by making this as easy as possible, you are more likely to stick to the practice daily. We followed his recommendation to answer 3 simple questions each day.

How it works

When you start each day with journalling, it is shown to have many benefits, such as improved sleep, reduced anxiety and depression, easier to turn new behaviors into long-term behaviors and enhanced relationships - ultimately helping us to lead more mindful and

EMBRACE

intentional lives.

To journal, you don't need a physical diary to write in. To make it accessible and easy I used a chalkboard that we have painted onto our kitchen wall. Dr Chatterjee recommends these 3 questions.

Question 1: What is the **most important thing** you have to do today?

- This acknowledges that not everything is equally important. It is not a to do list. It helps us to see through the busyness of our day and focus on what is really important to us. Usually, people tend to do important things *after* their to do list is completed.
- The important things in life are our relationships and our health. We often only squeeze them in when we have the time.
- This practice requires you to shift the focus of your brain, so that once you achieve that one important thing, you have had a successful day.
- It also helps you put intention and focus into your day.

Question 2: What **one thing** do I deeply appreciate about my life?

- Starting each morning by focusing on what you have in life rather than what you lack is positive and powerful. It is an antidote to our natural negativity bias.
- A study showed that after practicing 3 days of gratitude for 20 minutes each day, up to 3 months later, the people from the study were continuing to experience better moods, had less illness and had fewer visits to their doctor.
- There is a ton of research that shows the power of gratitude, and this simple question puts it at the start of every day.

Question 3: What **quality do I want to show** the world today?

- By regularly asking yourself this question, you learn more about yourself and it will start to change the way you experience each day.
- It is a powerful way of intentionally deciding how you want to be in the world and how you want to show up.
- When we react, we are not being who we are. This question is powerful in that by taking a moment to think about it, you draw that into your awareness. **You become who you want to be, not who you think you are**.
- By asking yourself this question every day, you begin to reinforce the qualities that you want to have.

Our experience

This simple daily practice changed the energy of our household to one that was much more caring, compassionate and loving. While we kept it up for many weeks before it slowly started looking more and more empty, it undoubtedly made a positive impact on the whole family.

I liked that it reminded me daily of how much I love my family—how much I appreciate them and cherish them for who they are. I make it a point to tell both of my sons that I love them every day (sometimes, I even say it many times!).

However, trying to "think yourself better" is simply not working for Andy. I realize that for someone with severe depression, this notion can be insulting and hurtful, as it implies that their condition is their fault and that it's "easy" to fix. His depression is not improving; in fact, he has hit an all-time low.

One day, as I was encouraging him to jump on his mini trampoline, he broke down, crying out, "I hate being like this. I just want to be normal. I feel like I have a black cloud around me, and I can't get rid of it."

Light bulb moment

Oh my god. Why didn't I think of this sooner? It's an energy problem. Andy needs energy healing!

I'm into all this holistic stuff, and I can't believe it didn't occur to me earlier. I know there are skilled practitioners out there, but there are also some who aren't. I put it out to the universe, asking for help in finding a great energy healer.

I started Googling and found someone with excellent reviews who wasn't far from us and had availability.

Energy Healing / Reiki

What it is

The way I described this to Andy is by asking him where is his battery? What is it that keeps his heart pumping and his body going?

"Is that a trick question? I don't know." He replied.

"We are all energy. We are powered by our soul, which is energy. Energy moves and flows through our energy centers, known as Chakras. Energy can become stagnant, get blocked, be over or under powered in certain chakras. We can have energetic tears or leaks and other people can be energy vampires and take our energy from us."

In a nutshell, energy healing restores the flow of energy through our chakras.

How it works

An energy healer channels source energy into their patient to heal and restore energy. A good energy healer is also intuitive and will pick up information that helps to understand the energetic issues.

Our experience

The energy healer said that she felt it would be good for Andy to find the music he will resonate with for happier feelings, as the heavy metal music he currently listens to keeps him rooted in his anger, angst and negative emotions.

Andy had allowed me to stay in the room as she did the energy healing, so I tuned in and meditated while she worked. I received an insight that in order to heal, Andy needs to forgive the bullies from primary school. He needs to let go of that anger and hurt. We spoke about it afterwards and he felt he was not ready yet, however, he did understand that it is important to do.

Andy enjoyed the session and felt good afterwards. He said he would like to do energy healing again.

For half the cost of a psychologist, I felt that we got a lot more bang for our buck with an energy healing session.

Frequency of love

What it is

My love and appreciation for Andy is immense. I know that positive affirmations were not for him, but I felt strongly that immersing him in love and positivity was important. At the risk of sounding soft, I believe that love is the answer to many of life's problems, and I planned to surround him with love.

I subscribe to Gaia TV, which 'supports the global evolution of consciousness.' I find that when I watch programs on Gaia, I feel like I am consuming food for my soul. In my opinion, this is what we should be teaching kids in school – topics such as sacred geometry, the science of sound, the limits of human potential, the universe, energy and spirituality to empower ourselves.

For those who have not heard of sacred geometry, it is the study of all of the patterns behind everything in existence, with the understanding that it was bought about by higher consciousness. There is an invisible energetic pattern behind everything in physical creation. Through sacred geometry we can find the interconnectedness of all things. The Fibonacci spiral is an example of sacred geometry, as it shows the same geometric pattern and mathematical order of petals on a flower, to the structure of galaxies – and also our ear is a Fibonacci spiral!

It was while I was watching a program called 'The Sound of Creation', which wove together my favorite topics of sacred geometry, energy and healing, that I decided to play frequency music to Andy. I played it while he slept, particularly during the period between sleeping and waking up, to help align his own frequency to a higher vibration and thus lift him out of his denser, more negative energetic state.

It is very simple to do, search YouTube for "high-frequency music" to help with whatever it is you are looking for; Healing, removing toxins, clearing energy, spiritual growth, pain relief or manifesting. It is all there, plus more.

How it works

Everything is energy

Energy vibrates at different frequencies

Love and gratitude are high frequencies (and closer to source energy)

Depression, anger, jealousy and hate are dense, low-frequency energies (not good).

When you listen to a sound with a certain frequency, your brain waves synchronize with it. Therefore, by playing high-frequency music, being grateful for Andy and loving him consciously every day, we are raising his frequency and helping to shift his focus from anger to love.

Our experience

Playing frequency music is an important part of his healing which is now a daily practice in our home. I will often put on high frequency music in the background during the day as well. I have recently discovered light code language, which is an energetic form of communication that we feel. It also lifts our frequency to a higher vibration and can be used to heal.

I have found that light language is a bit more energetic and upbeat, so I tend to play this during the day, and have been sticking to the high-frequency music in the mornings. If I was going to play music while I meditated, I would choose a high-frequency playlist over light language.

Part 2: Healing

Chapter 12
Energy Healing Hub

One day while Andy and I were driving to an energy healer, we both simultaneously noticed a sign for the "Energy Healing Hub." We had driven down this road so many times before and never spotted it, but in that moment, it was like something invisible turned both our heads at the same time.

Without missing a beat, Andy said, "I want to go there."

I looked at the sign and replied, "That logo is sacred geometry! It's the flower of life. We have to go there."

And it is at this point that we genuinely got on the road to recovery. The black clouds were about to be blown away.

Energy Enhancement System (EES)

What it is

Developed by Dr. Sandra Rose Michael, The Energy Enhancement System combines body, mind, spirit and quantum physics to give us the ultimate fuel for our bodies, improving circulation and oxygenation and increasing cellular energy to reach higher states of health, consciousness and self-actualization. In simple terms, like a battery charger for your cells.

How does it work?

EES is a technology that uses custom-installed computers to create energy fields that can be beneficial for your body. These energy fields can help your cells regenerate, reduce inflammation, boost your immune system, reduce pain, detoxify your body, improve your mood, and balance the left and right sides of your brain to give you more energy.

"It does this by generating scalar waves. A scalar wave is a fifth-dimensional non-linear wave. They are unbounded and capable of passing through solid matter.

When the human body enters a scalar wave field, the electromagnetic field of the individual becomes excited. This catalyzes the mind/body complex to return to a more optimal state. Cells in the human body, when functioning at its maximum health potential, range between 70-90 millivolts. Disease and aging occur when the cellular energy depreciates to levels below this range. Every cell has a crystalline structure that is capable of holding a charge. The non-linear (Scalar) waves move through the matrix of the body via the crystalline structures within each cell. This charge begins the process of increasing the cell's millivolt range and cellular regeneration. As the cells are charged, any toxins in the cell begin to be released. Research has indicated that exposure to scalar fields can involve DNA repair."

Source: wholenesshealing.com

"The power that made the body, heals the body"

Dr. Sandra Rose Michael

Our experience

The results were immediate and I could see him clearly for the first time in a long time. He shone. All the teachers at school the following day commented on how good he looked. I cried with happiness. We were on the healing path we needed to be on.

I scheduled two more sessions at the Energy Healing Hub, spaced two weeks apart. While the follow-up sessions didn't have the same profound impact as the first one, that first session really pulled Andy out of his darkest place. Still, every time we went into the Energy Enhancement System (EES), Andy emerged stronger, with more of his true self shining through.

The Energy Healing Hub is run by Suzy and Ken Elias. Suzy is an incredibly gifted energy healer, psychic, and medium. When booking EES sessions, there's an option to have Suzy perform energy healing on you while you're in the room. I always chose this option for Andy, as he needed all the support he could get.

During these sessions, Suzy doesn't speak to you—you just lie down, relax for two hours in a big comfy recliner, and she quietly moves around the room. At the end, she leaves written notes about what she healed, along with any insights she received. In our first session, Suzy picked up on energetic tears caused by bullying, which had weakened Andy's inner power and self-esteem in his solar plexus chakra. She also noted lower digestive discomfort and gut irritability, along with other comments that were incredibly accurate. The fact that she could gather all this information without even speaking to us was absolutely amazing.

After three two-hour EES sessions, I wanted a more personal experience with Suzy, where we could interact and ask questions directly. In the EES, Suzy works with up to four or five other people, but in a one-on-one session, she focuses solely on you for an entire hour. She truly is the most gifted energy healer I've encountered.

During our private session, Suzy asked Andy what he wanted to know, and then tuned into his higher self to provide the answers he was seeking.

Andy had two questions:

- Why am I the way I am?
- How do I get better?

Suzy spent a few minutes tuning into Andy's higher self, quietly writing down the messages she received. Then she put down her pen and began sharing everything we needed to know to help him.

She explained that Andy is the way he is due to heavy metal toxins in his brain, and emphasized that there is nothing wrong with his spirit or soul. However, his physical and energetic bodies need additional support.

She then instructed us to do the following.

- Buy Anthony Williams's medical Medium book called Brain Saver. His books contain all the information you need to know about detoxing heavy metals.
- Keep the energy in the home clean, place crystals around the house and play high-frequency music, also clear the energy in the house using a sage stick.
- Continue with EES and he will begin to feel more and more joy
- Energy transmutation and grounding

Suzy also shared that Andy is a teacher—here to teach mercy, love, and compassion. She explained that when people are around him, they are presented with the opportunity to choose these qualities. I love that!

Before we left, Suzy performed some energy healing on Andy. She had him lie down on a massage table and worked through his energy centers. As she called in angels and guides, the energy in the room shifted—it was incredible to witness.

Andy experienced a strong sense of déjà vu during the healing, which is often a sign of an energetic shift. It was truly an amazing experience (I've since had my own session with Suz, and I can say it feels even more powerful when it's done to you!).

"We all volunteer to be here, your mission is to remember who you are, heal and step into your power so you can share your higher consciousness and light with those who need it."

Suzy Elias

from the EES energy healing notes she wrote for Andy

Anthony Williams, Medical Medium

Who he is

Anthony was born with the unique ability to converse with the Spirit of Compassion, who provides him with extraordinarily advanced healing medical information that's far ahead of its time. In his #1 New York Times best-selling books **Brain Saver,** and **Brain Saver Protocols and Recipes**, he provides detailed information about the causes of neurological, mental health and immunodeficiency issues. In the Protocols and Recipes book, he provides information on how to detox the brain and what supplements are required to heal the brain for many, many ailments.

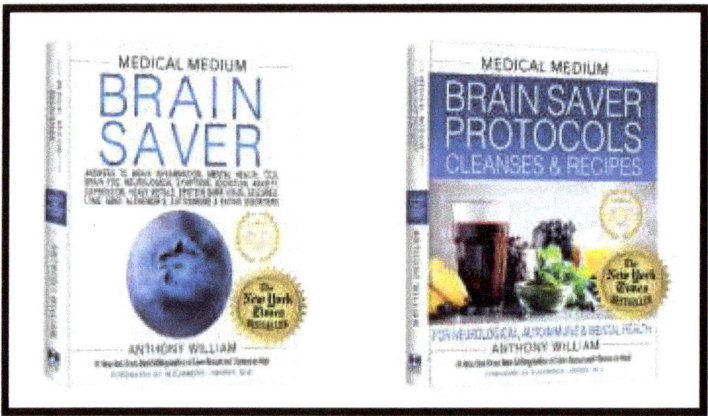

How he heals

No matter the issue, every protocol with Anthony starts the same way: with celery juice and a heavy metal detox smoothie. From there, you follow his recommendations on the necessary supplements. Anthony offers a supplement list tailored to a variety of neurological, autoimmune, and mental health concerns. For Andy, we began with his specific protocols for ADHD, autism, and depression.

Our experience

Anthony's knowledge is truly mind-blowing, and everything he says makes so much sense. Remember the naturopath when Andy was 8? The extreme toxic heavy metal results? Now, I'm reading detailed explanations of exactly why and how those metals are affecting him. The best part is that there's concrete information on how to help him get better! Every morning, Andy starts his day with celery juice, a heavy metal detox smoothie, and the supplements recommended for ADHD, autism, and depression. What I can tell you is that:

- Andy is now at school full-time and thriving.
- He has gone from resting his head on the desk for most of the day, to actively participating.
- He is much better in the afternoons, which is when he used to struggle the most
- Following a lemon balm shock therapy for depression, Andy had no desire to self-harm for the first time in a long time

Bonus: I also have his brother on the protocol for Seizures.

Some resistance

As we started the Medical Medium protocol, Andy began resisting the heavy metal detox smoothies and supplements. We had come so far, and it felt like we were really onto something. But he had reached his limit. One day, when I picked him up from school, the school counsellor asked for a quick chat. We discussed the protocol, and Andy expressed how much he didn't want to drink the smoothies anymore. She stepped in with an unbiased perspective and helped him see that it was worth sticking with. I'm so grateful she was there to mediate and help bridge the conversation between us.

I also want to take a moment to acknowledge the incredible effort and commitment Andy has put into getting better. He genuinely wanted to improve and was willing to do whatever it took. This journey has been long, and it's understandable that his patience started to wear thin. However, he clung in there, and I'm so proud of him for doing that.

Chapter 13

The End of Meds

As I mentioned, the EES and energy healing were a great help, but Andy was still struggling with feelings of depression. Then, one day, things really turned around. It was April 10, 2024, and Andy had a school excursion to the Sydney Aquarium. In the rush of getting myself ready for work and Andy out the door, I completely forgot to give him his medications. It wasn't until 2 p.m. that I realized, with a wave of panic. Oh no! I quickly called him...

"Andy, baby, are you ok?!"

"Yeah, why?"

"Oh my God, Andy, I totally forgot to give you your medications today. Are you alright?"

"I feel great, mum. In fact, I don't feel depressed at all. I'm having a great day. I can't remember the last time I felt this good."

It was a night for me and Google that evening. I researched all the medications he was on. He had been taking his medications for 4 years, so my research included the following:

- Long-term use of medications he was taking; and
- the effects of combining the medications he was taking, and
- uncommon side effects

What became clear to me that night was that the Concerta (for ADHD) had been the culprit all along. Andy hasn't taken another tablet since that day, and he's doing better now than when he was on the medication.

I believe the healing benefits of the EES, combined with the ongoing Medical Medium detoxing and supplements, have made the need for Concerta disappear. There's been absolutely no downside to him coming off it.

I kept Andy on Fluoxetine (for anxiety and depression) because I wanted to ensure he remained stable, and I knew this wasn't a medication you could stop abruptly—it required careful weaning. After consulting our GP, we reduced his dosage, planning to continue with one tablet a day until the pack ran out in a couple of months. However, it wasn't long before I started finding the tablets in the toilet or behind the couch. Andy had clearly decided that was the end of pharmaceuticals.

Now, Andy relies solely on natural supplements recommended by the Medical Medium. While we still encounter some bumps along the way, he's doing much better. He can now focus for a full day at school, which was previously a struggle. On all fronts—concentration, depression, anxiety, and behavior—he's doing far better than when he was on any pharmaceutical medication.

Chapter 14

Bumps in the road

Healing is definitely a process. While it felt like Andy had experienced an "overnight success," that light and happy feeling didn't last as long as I'd hoped. Almost immediately after he seemed to shed his depression, one of his close friends began struggling, and Andy quickly became their go-to support person. He even kept his phone by his bedside to be available in case they needed him throughout the night.

How did Andy go from being so deeply depressed to supporting someone else so quickly? Wow. I was incredibly proud of the caring, kind person he was becoming, but I couldn't help but worry for him.

Things started to spiral fast. He began self-harming again, and even mentioned to someone at school that he wanted to commit suicide. Suddenly, he had the classic teenage attitude—"No. No. No!" I was devastated.

Thankfully, Andy'sfriend got the support they needed and was able to put some distance between them. Within just two days, it was like the clouds lifted, and there he was—my darling Andy, coming back to us.

This highlighted for me how much constant diligence and effort it takes to keep Andy in a good state of mind, and how quickly and easily he can fall.

A few days later, I had just returned home from a relaxing, uplifting afternoon at the Energy Healing Hub. I'd barely been home for five minutes when there was a knock at the door.

"That'll be the groceries," I called out to my husband. He opened the door, only to find two uniformed police officers standing there in full gear.

We invited them in, and they sat in our living room. I was certain they were here to talk about Andy's friend....

"Is Andy living here?" They ask

"Yes, he does live here."

"We are here to conduct a wellbeing visit as we have received a call from the school who are concerned about Andy and some of the online content he has been viewing as well as being suicidal. We are here to talk to Andy and call in Paramedics if we feel he is at risk."

At that moment, you could have knocked me down with a feather—and trust me, you'd need to pick up all the pieces of my broken heart off the floor, too.

After a discussion with the police, it turned out that Andy had been talking to others about the disturbing content he had seen on the dark web. I won't go into details because, honestly, what he watched is irrelevant; it was illegal, and if he were over 18, he would be facing serious charges.

While the police determined he wasn't suicidal, they could see he wasn't in a great place, so they called in the paramedics. It felt like we were having a "triple zero" party in our little living room, packed with two uniformed police officers and three paramedics. What a Saturday night!

Andy spent a few minutes talking to the paramedics and opened up about more details regarding his friendship. The friend who had been struggling had been sending photos of themselves self-harming, which triggered memories of what Andy had seen on the dark web. He was grappling with ongoing intrusive thoughts, pulling him back to some dark places. He mentioned this at school, and they had reported it.

Having police and paramedics in my house because my son had accessed illegal content on the dark web and was struggling with suicidal thoughts felt terrible. Once I started crying, I couldn't stop.

EMBRACE

A part of me had been so relieved when his depression improved that I didn't know if I had the energy to deal with more. I felt exposed, like a bad parent and a failure. I was embarrassed. I wished he had spoken to me instead of the school counselor; I could have managed the situation if I had just known.

After they all left, I soaked in a very hot bath, put on some relaxing frequency music, and took a few deep breaths, trying to find my calm amidst the chaos.

I realized that the crying was my ego. This is not about me and I am not a bad parent. This is Andy's life and Andy's story. His journey isn't yet finished and so there are some more chapters to go before I can give you the story with the happy ending.

I won't give up!

Chapter 15

Empaths

Through this experience, I've come to realize that Andy is an empath. An empath is someone who has a heightened sensitivity and absorbs other people's energy like a sponge, often without even realizing it. This can lead to all sorts of unpleasant feelings, like depression, anxiety, and fatigue.

I doubt there's much empirical data on empaths, but I did find a couple of references suggesting that around 2% of the population might be classified as empaths. It's a small percentage, but it explains a lot about what Andy has been going through.

I believe Andy is an empath for the following reasons:
- I have seen him change after spending a short amount of time with certain people, in particular those who have mental health or behavioural issues. Andy's behaviour will tank badly after being with these types of people.
- Andy was in a good place after the energy healing sessions and suddenly fell off a cliff after spending time with someone who was depressed. They were self-harming and feeling suicidal. Andy began to self-harm and feel suicidal. He did not realise that wasn't his shit. He had absorbed it and taken it on as his own. As soon as he was removed from the friendship, he improved.
- When Andy sees someone hurting, he *feels* their hurt. He puts helping others before his own well-being.
- He loves solitude. It is safe and calm.
- Remember all the Houdini acts? He avoids crowded places. I can't imagine what it must feel like for him. I can't even take him out shopping for new clothes, as he won't come to a shopping centre. We do amazingly well on hand-me-downs.
- Andy feels emotions freely and deeply. Very deeply.

- He becomes distracted easily. This is obviously a part of having ADHD, but it is also a common trait for empaths, so I am including it here.
- He fatigues easily and after a day at school, he needs time to be alone and rest. This could also be attributed to Autism, as he needs to spend a lot more energy functioning throughout the day, resulting in a weary and tired Andy at the end of the day.
- People tell him their problems.

Since Andy's depression lifted, he has become quite popular among a few young people at school. They feel comfortable talking to him, and he loves it because he genuinely wants to help them. He understands that just by being there to listen, he can make a difference. With his deep empathy and kindness, he has become a magnet for kids who need a caring ear.

At a recent parent-teacher interview, the teachers couldn't stop praising Andy for his kindness. Seriously, kindness is his superpower! One of the most beautiful things we heard that evening was about one of Andy's friends who had come out of their shell this year. They credited Andy for their transformation, saying that his kind attention and friendship helped them go from not speaking at all to engaging openly. My heart is so full. I'm incredibly proud of him—my angel, my darling angel. My darling *teenage* angel.

"Don't go on about that chakra shit mum" [exaggerated eyeroll]

While I am so proud of Andy, I am also concerned. As you can see, it takes a toll and can send him backwards fast. When I woke up one day to find that he had self-harmed again, I immediately booked in another session with Suzy as well as an overnight in the Energy Enhancement System.

The session with Suzy was incredible. She found that he was blaming himself for not being able to help his friend.

Suzy was able to help him to understand that everyone has free will and his friend chose not to respond to the help he was trying to give. She gave him a power phrase **"I will help without the fear of failure."**

She also noted that Andy has a powerful heart energy and healed a self-love block, noting that he blames himself when others don't heal from his help. She gave him another power phrase: **"I am love."**

As soon as we got home, we wrote up the power phrases on a whiteboard and placed it in his room to remind him every day.

The energy healing is important to Andy, as he is so sensitive. He walked out of there glowing and skipped to the car!

How can we help Andy to manage being an empath

Funnily enough, the full list of recommendations given by Suzy is what I am using to manage Andy being an empath.

Pyramid of White Light

The pyramid of white light is also commonly known as the bubble or sphere of white light. However, being a sacred geometry nerd, I find the pyramid more powerful.

When I create the pyramid of white light, it's super simple and takes less than a minute. I tell Andy to picture a beautiful pyramid of white light that glows and sparkles. I ask him to place that pyramid around his body so that it completely encloses him. I explain that it's a powerful force that protects him, allowing positive energy to flow in while negative energy just bounces right off.

I use this technique, too! I place the pyramid of white light around my car while I drive, and I surround myself and my family with it as well. I really encourage anyone to try this out. It's not just imaginary; remember, everything is energy!

Transmutation and grounding

Here's another simple and quick method. When Andy gets home from school in the afternoon, I ask him to close his eyes and visualize any negative energy swirling around him. Then, he sends that energy spiraling down into the earth, which absorbs it all. Once that's done, he fills himself up with pure white light.

I try to get him to do this right on the doorstep before we head inside. Plus, taking a hot bath with sea salt really helps remove any energy he's picked up throughout the day. It's a great way to refresh and reset!

The use of crystals

Some people might see crystals as just pretty rocks, but I believe there's so much more to them than meets the eye. A quick read of Dolores Cannon or Sarah Breskman Cosme can give you some insight into the incredible, ancient power that crystals hold.

Regardless of what you believe, crystals are undeniably beautiful and can make any space feel calm and clear. And if their effects come from the placebo effect, who cares? Whatever works! I absolutely love our crystals.

We've placed selenite on our windowsills and above our front door. It's known for promoting peace, calm, mental clarity, and overall well-being, plus it helps to remove negative energy.

Andy wears a black obsidian crystal around his neck every day. This stone is fantastic for protecting against negative energy, psychic attacks, and other harmful vibes. It helps him stay grounded and shielded.

I've also put a few clear quartz crystals in both of my son's rooms, as they're known for their healing properties and supporting spiritual growth. Smoky quartz is another favorite in Andy's room;

it's a protective stone that counters fear, helps overcome depression, and brings emotional stability.

Lastly, we have a beautiful amethyst in his room. This stone is all about peace and is believed to help with anxiety, depression, and mental clarity.

❤ ❤ ❤ ❤

After the Triple 0 party at our house, I decided to reconnect with the psychologist we had previously seen. We had only had two sessions with her before Andy's miraculous recovery from depression, so it felt good to pick up where we left off. The great news was that she could see a significant improvement in Andy!

We initially started seeing her because she specializes in a treatment called EMDR, which I thought would be helpful for Andy in processing some of the disturbing content he had come across.

EMDR

What it is

Eye Movement Desensitization and Reprocessing (EMDR) is a psychotherapy that enables people to heal from the symptoms and emotional distress that are the result of disturbing life experiences. (source: EMDR Institute Inc). I felt that it might help with Andy's intrusive thoughts and the trauma of seeing the disturbing online content. I also felt there was an opportunity for Andy to process the trauma from the bullying in primary school.

How it works

It requires the patient to focus on the traumatic experience while simultaneously experiencing bilateral stimulation through eye movement, which is associated with a reduction in the emotion associated with the traumatic memories.

"Eye movements (or other bilateral stimulation) are used during one part of the session. After the clinician has determined which memory to target first, he asks the client to hold different aspects of that event or thought in mind and to use his eyes to track the therapist's hand as it moves back and forth across the client's field of vision. As this happens, for reasons believed by a Harvard researcher to be connected with the biological mechanisms involved in Rapid Eye Movement (REM) sleep, internal associations arise and the clients begin to process the memory and disturbing feelings.

In successful EMDR therapy, the meaning of painful events is transformed on an emotional level. For instance, a rape victim shifts from feeling horror and self-disgust to holding the firm belief that, "I survived it and I am strong." Unlike talk therapy, the insights clients gain in EMDR therapy result not so much from clinician interpretation, but from the client's own accelerated intellectual and emotional processes.

The net effect is that clients conclude EMDR therapy feeling empowered by the very experiences that once debased them. Their wounds have not just closed. They have transformed. As a natural outcome of the EMDR therapeutic process, the client's thoughts, feelings and behavior are all robust indicators of emotional health and resolution—all without speaking in detail or doing homework used in other therapies."

Source: EMDR Institute Inc.

Our experience

Andy had three EMDR sessions when his wonderful psychologist realized that this was not the therapy to help Andy.

To help Andy tackle the intrusive thoughts, his psychologist assigned him some daily homework. This involves him sitting with those unsettling thoughts for a while and either writing or drawing what he's experiencing. Once he's done, we burn the paper with his drawings. This process is meant to gradually desensitize him, so the thoughts lose their power and stop popping up.

By sticking to this daily routine, along with the Medical Medium's shot therapy for intrusive thoughts—made from radish, sage leaves, apple, and celery— it took about 6 to 8 weeks for the thoughts to diminish to a point where they no longer bothered him.

❤ ❤ ❤ ❤

Chapter 16

Quantum Healing Hypnosis Technique

(QHHT)

Discovering Dolores

The late Dolores Cannon developed an incredible hypnosis technique called Quantum Healing Hypnosis Technique (QHHT), honed over decades of working with thousands of clients. This specific technique combines past-life regression with subconscious contact to facilitate healing. It's fascinating how much energetic residue we carry from our past lives into our current existence, often manifesting in our bodies and lives in unexpected ways.

I've always been captivated by the power of the mind and the healing potential of hypnosis, particularly past-life regression. When I was a teenager, I read Many Lives, Many Masters by Dr. Brian Weiss. It's a well-known book about a psychiatrist trying to help a young woman struggling with various issues and phobias. After exhausting all his techniques, he finally turned to hypnosis, allowing her to regress into past lives. This process was transformative for her healing and left a lasting impression on me.

In my final year of high school, I took a psychology unit where we watched a video about a woman covered head to toe in incurable psoriasis. She saw a hypnotist who used hypnosis to cure just one side of her body to prove that it was indeed hypnosis at work. Amazingly, she cleared up completely on the one side. But don't worry, once they proved their point, they healed her other side too. How cool is that?

After a couple of years of casual work post-high school, I decided to pursue a Diploma in Clinical Hypnotherapy and Counselling. I absolutely loved it! The course was fascinating, and I learned so much about counseling, hypnosis, and myself. With a small class, it felt like being part of a fun therapy group for a couple of years.

Once I completed the course and started seeing clients, I quickly realized that being in my twenties meant I lacked the life experience necessary to help people through their challenges, so I put hypnotherapy on the back burner. I spent the next 25 years enjoying corporate life, primarily in project work, and surprisingly, my background in hypnotherapy and counseling proved more helpful than I expected.

I follow Suzy on Instagram [@meditatewithsuz], and one day she posted a quote from a book that instantly caught my attention. I downloaded the book on Audible that day: A Hypnotist's Journey from the Trail to the Star People by Sarah Breskman-Cosme. I finished it in just two days—it changed me.

Sarah is a QHHT practitioner, and her book was based on sessions with a client who had lived as a Native American during the Trail of Tears. The story was incredibly moving, and the information blew my mind. After diving into numerous books by both Dolores Cannon and Sarah Breskman-Cosme, I realized I was hooked. This topic fascinates me endlessly, and I always knew I'd return to my first career in hypnosis after gaining some life experience. Now, as I approach 50, that time has finally arrived.

Plus, I might just be able to help Andy even more through this journey. If being drawn to these books like a super-powered magnet wasn't a strong enough sign, within a week, I received three clear signals that it was time to enroll in the QHHT course. I met a level 3 practitioner, then Suzy told me when I completed my studies that she would love me work at the Energy Healing Hub, then the final nudge was a 'solstice sale' that offered a significant discount on the course. It felt meant to be!

While I learned that QHHT isn't recommended for children—specifically those under 16 (and Andy is currently 15)—I completely understand and respect that past life regression isn't something for kids. But not all hope is lost! There is a way to facilitate healing for children through QHHT using a surrogate, which gives me hope for Andy's journey.

What happens in a QHHT session

A QHHT session typically lasts a minimum of four hours and can extend up to six hours. However, it's important to note that the hypnosis portion will never exceed two hours. The first two to three hours—or even longer—is dedicated to the Interview. During this time, we dive deep into the client's current life, exploring health issues, life events, relationships, and anything else that comes up. This step is crucial, as it helps identify patterns that might be affecting their life.

Only after the Interview do we transition into the hypnosis phase, where past life regression takes place. While in hypnosis, we can access profound subconscious information and facilitate healing.

Before a session, clients are encouraged to prepare a list of questions. These can relate to anything, but they often focus on life purpose, relationships, career, and health. If healing is needed via surrogate, the client simply formulates a question for their subconscious to address the healing for the surrogate.

QHHT via surrogate

Suzy had identified some past life responsibility blocks in Andy that seemed tied to his feelings of failing the people he helps. I wanted to see if we could address this through QHHT via surrogate.

To become a QHHT practitioner, I first needed to experience it as a client myself. So, I eagerly booked a session and prepared a list of questions to explore during the session. One of my main goals was to understand and confirm the purpose behind Andy's issues and, of course, to request healing for him.

The result

The information I received from my higher self during my session:

- Andy is 'an experience hunter' and is therefore drawn to challenging situations in order to experience them. He feels so intensely and has attracted such dark experiences. It has, at times, been almost too much.
- However, through his experience he has shown me the way, that there are better avenues of healing. The energetic healing modalities help people to evolve, rather than by simply masking their symptoms (which is a part of their true self) with pharmaceuticals.
- We need to help people understand how to heal without drugs, and to show that when you heal with energy and love, you release your inner power, inner strength and while doing so, continuing to evolve to your highest potential.
- The power to heal is within everyone, the power is not in a tablet. The power is in **you**.
- This helps with the ascension of earth because this is teaching people to be their true selves.
- It is also his purpose to help others. He will experience so much love as he gets older. He will inspire young people, they will see him as being so cool and look up to him as a role model.

- Andy's experience is helping people to accept themselves for who they are. He hated being different but as he embraces that, he will realise that it is his greatest gift.

When healing for Andy was requested, I saw a Merkaba around his body.

The Merkaba gets its name from three components: Mer for light, Ka for spirit, and Ba for the body. It's a sacred geometric shape made up of two tetrahedrons, one pointing up and the other down. These tetrahedrons symbolize the masculine and feminine energies within us, rotating in opposite directions to create balance and stability. The Merkaba can be a powerful tool for spiritual connection and deep healing.

I believe that the Merkaba surrounding Andy's body indicated that energies were helping to align and balance his spiritual and physical selves.

Chapter 17

Andy Today

Today, as I look back and reflect on how far Andy has come in just six months, it feels nothing short of a miracle. I can hardly believe I'm looking at the same person! We've had our ups and downs, but his progress is consistently upward, with just a few dips along the way. It's more like up, up, up, dip, up, up, dip—definitely not a rollercoaster ride!

Where he once struggled to engage in conversation and felt completely drained, today he wakes up excited for school. He smiles, laughs, and chats with the family over dinner, sharing stories about his good days at school. He regularly jumps on his rebounder without needing any prompts to exercise! He's decided to eat healthier and cut sugar out of his diet. He recently applied for a job at KFC; unfortunately, he didn't get it, but I'm thrilled that he feels ready to take on a job! He's genuinely excited about working, which is something we never even dreamed of discussing six months ago.

We're also keeping up with our overnight sessions in the Energy Enhancement System whenever we can, helping Andy feel stronger and more empowered in his abilities. Recently, we've incorporated a daily mantra recommended by Bashar, channeled through Darryl Anka (@basharchanneling). Bashar says the most powerful mantra for humans is:

"I am who I am, and that is enough."

He suggests saying it three times upon waking and three times before bed. It's been a beautiful addition to our routine, and I do it too—give it a shot! It's so simple yet incredibly powerful.

Whenever Andy has a dip, we just book a private session with Suzy. He always feels fantastic after those energy-healing sessions.

I'm also incredibly happy and relieved to share that we can enjoy holidays as a family again. It's so much fun to be able to take walks, play board games, and truly relax away from home—without the Xbox! These moments together are so precious, and I'm grateful to have them back.

Summary of approaches and therapies that contributed to healing

You might have noticed by now just how complex Andy is. We've explored a wide range of therapies to support him, and each has contributed in its own way to address specific issues.

To provide a bit of clarity on this journey, I've put together a summary of how each therapy has helped. I've separated healing from management because they serve different purposes, and both are essential. Managing day-to-day life is crucial, but I really want everyone to keep healing in mind as well.

I've also highlighted the importance of the approach we've taken on his healing journey. Some of these methods are vital for helping him stay equipped to cope with the world and live the happy, fulfilling life that every parent wishes for their child.

Approach	How it helped Andy	Required to manage	Required to heal	Continue for maintenance
LENS	I understand this can be an effective intervention, but in our case, it had little effect, and the effect it did have, didn't last very long.	No	No	No
Naturopath	Helped in the management of gastrointestinal issues and leg sores. Early identification of toxic heavy metals in system, however the detoxing we undertook was not effective enough to see any changes.	Yes	Possibly, if given enough time	No
Social Work	A very important and pivotal stage of our journey. The therapy was helpful, and Rachel was the first person to see that	Yes	No	No

EMBRACE

	Andy had Autism and ADHD.			
Psychiatry	Gave us the diagnosis and medications to help manage day-to-day life.	Yes	No	No
Speech Therapy	Very helpful to assist with managing day-to-day life.	Yes	No	No
Tomatis	I wish I could give this therapy a better review, but I would only recommend this if you have NDIS funding or spare cash. It did help Andy, but unfortunately it did not heal him, which was our hope.	No	No	No
Psychologist	This initially had limited effectiveness for Andy, but when we found the right psychologist, we had much better results.	Yes	No	Yes
CYMHS	Brief interaction only, however they gave him the suicide prevention plan, which he used. CYMHS may have saved his life.	Yes	No	No
A school environment that caters to the needs of your child	It was so important to get him in the right environment to learn. It has been a significant step in his healing journey, and he is very happy at school - where he is accepted, supported and safe.	Yes	Yes	Yes
Brain hub	Re-programmed his neural pathways to assist with his biggest behavioral issues of impulse control and inability to sleep.	Yes	Yes	No
Energy healing (with Suzy)	Major reset – cleared all the negative energy away and healed energetic issues. Put us on the path	Yes	Yes	Yes

	to true and long-term healing.			
Energy Enhancement System (EES) – the overnight sessions	Critical in strengthening his energy so that he can maintain his mental health and energic clarity. Allows us to continue the upward trajectory. Helping him to become his true self and step into his inner power.	Yes	Yes	Yes
Medical medium	Significant contributing factor in being able to end pharmaceutical medications and eliminate toxic heavy metals from his system. This is a long game and we have incorporated the heavy metal detox program into our daily routine.	Yes	Yes	Yes
Ending pharmaceutical medications	Removed key toxic pharmaceuticals contributing to the depression	Yes	No	To be avoided
High frequency music, pyramid of light, transmutation, hot sea salt baths and crystals	Subtle, yet important to lift and maintain energy to higher frequency of light and love. Important in managing him being an empath, by protecting and clearing his energy daily.	Yes	Yes	Yes
EMDR	This was not appropriate therapy for Andy.	No	No	No
QHHT via surrogate	Provided insightful information and gave further understanding. Healing impact was subtle.	No	Yes	No

"Sensitivity is a gift and a superpower, not a hindrance. We are all sensitive, some people are just more tuned into it and when you emanate sensitivity in a harsh world, then you give others hope."
A Hypnotists Journey from the Trail to the Star People

Part 3:
Learning from the
Journey

Chapter 18

What I have learned

My journey with Andy has been a long and emotional one. We never stop learning, and in the past six months, I feel like I've been on an accelerated learning path. Here, I'm excited to share my insights and discoveries with you.

As a result of what I've been learning, my outlook on life has shifted. I feel much more at ease and open to "going with the flow" while trusting in the universe. I've even re-established a daily meditation practice—something I used to do regularly but paused during COVID when I lost my commute, which had been my meditation time.

Here, I share three important learnings which have become clear for me over the past six months:

1. Every life has a purpose, and every challenge a lesson
2. Anxiety is increasing because we are no longer in alignment with our inner truth as we evolve and ascend
3. Pharmaceuticals are overused and our environment is too toxic

Just a quick note: I'm not a scholarly expert by any means. I've become knowledgeable through experience, so I hope you enjoy my musings and find something that resonates with you. My experiences with Andy, along with my recent dive into QHHT and past life regression, have significantly shaped my perspective.

MARNIE JURKOWSKI

♥ ♥ ♥ ♥

In August 2024, Sarah Breskman-Cosme released the recording of her QHHT session with Robert Edward Grant on YouTube. I can hardly find the words to describe how I felt while listening to this incredible session—it was mind-blowing, to say the least! There were so many insights Robert shared that resonate deeply as absolute truths for me, capturing concepts I've been trying to convey in this book. He articulated them perfectly, so I've included several quotes from the session in the section below that I believe hold significant importance for our healing journey. If you apply these insights to your own path, I'm sure they'll help you embrace your unique journey and find healing too.

Be sure to check out the resources section for a link to the full recording—I highly recommend giving it a listen!

Chapter 19
Every Life Has a Purpose

Every life has a purpose, and every challenge a lesson

It doesn't matter who you are, where you were born, or the circumstances you were born into—every life has a purpose, and we all have lessons we have chosen to learn in this lifetime. Indeed, some lives are much more challenging than others, and that is all a part of each soul's evolution. You may look at someone who is having an easy life and wonder why they have it so easy compared to someone else. Maybe, they had a very challenging life prior to this (or will be having one soon), and this is a rest life. You just don't know, and it is not your place to judge others in this way.

As a QHHT practitioner, I've come to understand that we've all lived countless lives, each with its own unique purpose and lessons designed to advance our soul's evolution.

You may have heard the saying, "We are all one, and the one is all." The source of our soul energy is what some people refer to as God, or as I prefer to call it, simply "Source." I imagine Source as a massive ball of energy, with each of us as individual splinters sent out to experience life on Earth. Since we all come from the same source energy, we are interconnected—so when we harm others, we are, in a way, harming ourselves. When we hate others, we are hating ourselves. For some reason we have created a world full of separation, when in essence we are all one.

Reflecting on my own experience, when I was frustrated with Andy's difficult behaviors, I was really frustrated with my inability to respond in a calm, loving way. That was a lesson I needed to learn.

We make contracts with the people in our lives on the spirit side before we enter our current life, so that we can fulfil our life purpose and learn the lessons our soul needs to learn to progress on its journey to ascension.

Looking back on Andy's journey, and how we've navigated it together, I can see now that we were meant to go through this. All those times I cried when he was younger, wishing for an easier child—if only I had known then how fulfilling this journey would become! After all, how can you grow without challenges?

As Robert Edward Grant said during his QHHT session: "Suffering is not suffering, but a divine experience of the chosen path."

People often tell me how lucky Andy is to have me as his mum, given that I understand energy healing and am open to alternative approaches like the Medical Medium. But I have carried a lot of guilt from those early days, when my reactions were often filled with anger. Andy saw me struggle, cry, and lose my patience many times. I can't help but feel that contributed to his depression in his early teens, and that's a heavy burden to bear.

I've been very open with Andy about this. He knows I'm sorry for having been angry, and he knows I love him with all my heart. I've thanked him for helping me become a better person. I've reassured him that none of it was his fault—it was my ignorance in not knowing how to help him at the time.

Andy has helped me grow in so many ways. He's taught me to let go—of material things and of worrying about what others think. As long as we have each other and love each other, nothing else truly matters. He has brought so much joy into our lives. Despite the challenges, he is the funniest and most endearing boy. Even during his toughest times at school, at home he was a delight.

Finding the Energy Healing Hub felt like destiny. Both Andy and I were drawn to it at the same time, and we instantly knew we had to go there. Since starting this journey, Andy is a completely different person than when we first walked into that place.

Robert Edward Grant captured it beautifully when he said: "It is not important to ask why something happened, but rather, why did the observer choose to experience what he/she decided to experience as an individual unit of Source creation?"

I believe Andy's soul needed to go through these challenges to fulfill his life purpose of educating and helping others. These experiences have given him "superpowers"—he's become incredibly kind, caring, and compassionate as he's stepped into his own power.

I don't worry about Andy's future in the traditional sense. I trust the universe will take care of him. I'm already so proud of who he is and what he's achieved. It doesn't matter if he goes to university or has a high-profile career—he's already successful in the ways that truly matter. He helps others, and that is the ultimate measure of success.

Interestingly, in numerology, Andy's life path number is 22, considered the most powerful number. It combines the imagination of 2, the practicality of 4, and the insight of 11. People with this number often achieve great success but aren't motivated by personal glory—they're here to be of service to humanity. That is so Andy.

Through Andy's journey, I've also found my purpose. I now understand that his challenges were not just for his soul's growth, but also for mine. We agreed to this journey together, and by helping him and doing the EES with Andy, I have been becoming more and more in tune and aware of my own life purpose and have a greater connection to my higher self. While Andy is helping others who are going through their own tough time, I am writing this book to help the parents and have become a QHHT practitioner so I can help others heal.

Our life purpose is to go through these experiences and share them. Andy has taught me how to move through pain and heal with love. He has taught me the power of embracing our challenges. I've let go of guilt because it no longer serves me. I've learned my lesson, and now I can love and thank that experience for what it taught me and move forward.

Remember, everyone's journey is unique. No matter how hard it may seem, you chose this life and the people in it. Find your purpose. Learn the lessons your soul needs. And if you're struggling, ask for guidance—there's so much available to us if we just ask. Everyone has access to their higher self, and if you're not yet able to quiet your mind and listen, someone like Suzy or a QHHT practitioner can help you connect.

Chapter 20

The Ascension

Anxiety is increasing because we are no longer in alignment with our inner truth as we evolve

I don't believe we can point to a single cause for the rise in issues like depression and anxiety. There are several factors at play here, such as the influence of technology and social media, chemicals in our food, and the state of our environment with climate change. But I'd like to propose another contributing factor that's often overlooked: society's narrow definition of what is "normal" and "successful."

The earth is evolving. As we move toward the 5th dimension, the traditional ideas of success—like good grades, university degrees, popularity, and financial wealth—are becoming outdated. Were they ever true measures of success in the first place?

Before I go on, some of you may be scratching your head and wondering what on earth am I talking about? What is this shift from 3D to 5D?

As I said earlier, I'm not an expert and there are plenty of resources relating to this topic of which I have included a couple in the recommended reading section. However, I did feel it was important to include in this book because it is a significant learning for me. I will do my best to describe it without sounding too 'woo-woo'.

3D to 5D ascension

While every life has a purpose and lessons, the ultimate goal is to grow and evolve so we can achieve ascension. Put very simply, we ascend by increasing our frequency.

Earth is a living entity and has its own consciousness.

Earth is in a process of ascension too.

In order to ascend, Earth needs the consciousness of people to awaken and raise their frequency.

Feelings hold frequencies. Experiment with me and for a moment feel really, really angry or try to think of something you despise. Notice how that feels in your body. When I feel those emotions, I want to clench my fists and my jaw. It is a dense and heavy emotion (i.e. low frequency). Now think of something you love, feel and sit in gratitude for something or someone in your life. How does that feel? I feel light, it makes me sigh a big, gentle breath and I literally feel lighter (i.e. high frequency). So we can raise our frequency by focusing on and holding high frequency emotions like love and gratitude.

These are very interesting times. We are currently experiencing a spiritual evolution of humanity. Indeed, 5D is already here, as this is a personal and internal process. While some people will choose not to go on this ascension path, that is ok. Those who choose to ascend will do so by choosing love. In a nutshell, 3D is separation and 5D is living in unity, understanding that we are truly all one and not separate.

I suggest that many people feel depressed or anxious because they're not living in alignment with their own truth. We're pressured to conform to a limited version of success that might not resonate with who we really are.

I believe that this will become more and more apparent as people expand their consciousness and realize that the old ways are not giving them the satisfaction in life they had thought it would bring.

What we should be teaching our children is that true success comes from living with an open heart, filled with love and compassion. It's about being connected to nature, nurturing your spirituality, finding peace in stillness, and understanding your own energy. It's about protecting your energetic field and feeling accepted, supported, and safe to follow your own path, regardless of society's expectations.

For those on the autism spectrum, this is especially important. These are incredibly beautiful, sensitive souls who feel everything deeply—like having their emotions and thoughts laid bare for the world. They absorb everything around them. What they need most is to be nurtured, supported, and loved for who they are, without the pressure to fit into a box that doesn't reflect their unique essence.

Let's embrace a broader, more compassionate definition of success—one that allows everyone to thrive in their own way.

I recently listened to a podcast on Next Level Soul (great podcast if you are looking for a good one!), where Alex Ferrari was interviewing Suzy Miller, author of Awesomism: A new way to understand the diagnosis of autism (which, by the way, I wish I had known about back when Andy got his diagnosis). In this podcast, Suzy talks about the spiritual role these children play. Bingo! I knew it! These souls are here for a higher purpose.

Suzy Miller says that these kids come in at a higher frequency, and this rubs up against those places that are not integrated within ourselves, and this gives us opportunities to learn and grow (if we meet it with the right frame of mind of course).

This got me pondering that maybe the 'bully beacon' that I referred to earlier is actually Andy reflecting back an aspect of the bully to themselves that they don't like, so in effect, they are 'triggered' by the way they feel when they are with him.

For example, a bully may see vulnerability when they look at Andy, and this makes them feel uncomfortable because this is something they have an internal issue with, and so they want to attack Andy's vulnerability. But in fact, we all know that bullies are the most vulnerable people out there! Their tough exterior is just that, an exterior, and they are unable to tolerate anything that would show weakness in them and signify how psychologically fragile they are.

I was talking with Andy recently about how through suffering we grow and learn. He had an impressive understanding of this concept and can now see that the relentless and cruel bullying he experienced in primary school has made him who he is today. He is finally ready to forgive and embrace that part of his experience. By embracing that experience, he has blossomed the opposite within himself, which is loving, accepting and respecting of others.

Suzy Miller also says that "parents should not listen to every professional out there who tells you what your child is not. Let's find people who tell you what your child is. Difference versus disorder. Then you start to value the difference. Value your child for their uniqueness. Let's look at what they are doing, rather than what they are not."

I love the reframing and new perspective this gives! I also believe that currently, there are many souls being born to help Earth with its ascension. Andy is one of these.

If you have a sensitive soul in your family, and this book has found its way to you, then your child is likely here for the purpose to help raise our consciousness. That is very, very important and it is very, very special.

"Humanity agreed to experience this shift occurring at the planetary level, meaning that Mother Gaia, Earth, is shifting along with all on and within it. The experience of coherence, of being in sync with the Earth's growth, is the New Earth. It is a new expression for humankind."

Destination New Earth

Chapter 21

Too Many Toxins

Pharmaceuticals are overused and our environment is too toxic

As someone who has asthma, I'm fully aware that I owe my life to modern medicine, and I want to be clear—I'm not against vaccinations. However, through learning more about QHHT, I've come to understand that our bodies send us important messages through illness, aches, and pains. When we simply medicate symptoms and carry on with life, we're often ignoring the messages our body is trying to communicate, missing out on valuable lessons for our soul's growth.

In a QHHT session, we aim to uncover the deeper cause of illness, while traditional medicine often focuses more on symptom relief. This can lead to long-term dependence on pharmaceuticals, many of which contain toxins that can, over time, do more harm than good.

Take Andy's case, for example. The Concerta helped him focus in school and made life more manageable at home. But over time, it also contributed to his depression. If I could go back, I'd likely still start him on the medication, as we were desperate for help at the time. But I would've had a shorter-term plan. Reflecting now, I realize I would have gone straight to the Energy Healing Hub to address the root cause of his issues, rather than just masking the symptoms.

There's definitely a place for pharmaceuticals, and they can be life-saving. My point is that we need to stay mindful of how medicine is helping us (through symptom relief) and continue seeking the underlying causes. It's about identifying and releasing any energetic residue from past or present life traumas, so we can truly heal and move forward on our soul's journey.

I think an important aspect of this is removing as many toxins from your environment as possible. In our modern lives, there are so many toxins everywhere! The ease and accessibility to junk food (don't get me started on energy drinks), artificial fragrances in everything from household cleaning products, to beauty products and candles. Vapes! My gosh, it scares me to think what the cumulative effects of these are doing to our kids – and us adults.

Regardless of if you believe in Medical Medium or spirituality, it is common sense and critical to the health of our children that we keep our homes free of toxins as much as possible. If you could do one single thing to clean up your home of toxins, I recommend removing anything containing artificial fragrance. Artificial fragrances are unregulated and when you think how many products we use which have these toxins that we rub on our body, wash our hair, style our hair, wash our clothes, wash our hands, put into our atmosphere by way of air freshener, we are getting a lot of nasties.

The good news is that it is easier than ever to find great, environmentally friendly and fragrance-free replacements for all of these products. If you love candles and scented things, just make sure you buy those with essential oils and not artificial fragrance.

❤ ❤ ❤ ❤

Chapter 22

Final Thoughts

I have never seen Andy so excited and happy as when I told him that this book was to be published and that his story would be able to help others. He never even thought about hiding his identity or leaving out certain parts of his journey. He has always and unhesitatingly been overjoyed at the thought of helping others.

As I reflect on our journey, and as I myself learn more about the ascension process: what it means, what it is, how we experience it, I noticed one of the points of information I received during my QHHT session which at the time I didn't really understand:

- The power to heal is within everyone, the power is not in a tablet. The power is in you.

- This helps with the ascension of earth because this is teaching people to be their true selves.

I see now that Andy has healed in a way that is very much aligned with the fifth dimension. All the old ways simply didn't work for him. It wasn't until we used the energy enhancement system, specific and personal energy healing with Suzy and used natural ingredients to detox from heavy metals, did he start seeing visible and significant improvements.

Andy may just have shown us the future of healing. I am one, very, very proud mum who can't wait to see where Andy's journey takes him next!

Recommended Reading

QHHT

Soul Speak, The Language of your Body by Julia Cannon

The Three Waves of Volunteers and the New Earth by Dolores Cannon

A Hypnotist's Journey from the Trail to the Star People by Sarah Breskman Cosme

https://www.youtube.com/watch?v=Mm-7afUUhtA&t=1779s
QHHT session: Robert Edward Grant with Sarah Breskman Cosme

5D and the Ascension

Waking up in 5D: A Practical Guide to Multidimensional Transformation by Maureen J. St Germain

Destination New Earth, A blueprint to 5D consciousness by Alex Marcoux

Medical Medium

Medical Medium Brain Saver Protocols and Recipes, By Anthony Williams

Medical Medium Brain Saver, By Anthony Williams

Recommended Podcasts

Both Robert Edward Grant and Alex Ferrari have wonderful conversations with many interesting people on the topics I have covered in this book and more.

Think Tank, by Robert Edward Grant

Next Level Soul, by Alex Ferrari

About The Author

Marnie Jurkowski is a dedicated mother of two beautiful boys, Liam and Andy and they live together with her husband in Sydney, Australia.

Since childhood, Marnie has been fascinated and interested in spirituality and has practiced meditation daily for many years.

Marnie has had a corporate career in Change Management for the past 20 years, and often referred to herself as a 'hippy in corporate clothing' because she felt much more affiliation with nature rather than an office. However, being a people-person, she has been very happy and fulfilled, enjoying the opportunity to work with, and help so many wonderful people through corporate changes over the years.

In 2024, Marnie returned to her original career in hypnotherapy and counselling, by furthering her studies of healing through hypnosis, and she is now a Level 2 Quantum Healing Hypnosis Technique (QHHT) practitioner and works at the Sydney Energy Healing Hub.

With a unique blend of life experience and intuitive insight, Marnie is dedicated to guiding clients on their paths to self-discovery and healing. Through the powerful process of QHHT, she helps individuals connect with their inner wisdom, unlock hidden memories, and foster profound healing experiences that resonate on multiple levels.

When not working with clients, Marnie enjoys exploring the intersections of spirituality and personal growth, always eager to learn and share new insights. She believes that understanding our stories is key to healing and personal empowerment, and is passionate about helping others uncover the narratives that define them.

To book a session, go to www.sydneyenergyhealinghub.com.au

MARNIE JURKOWSKI

To follow Marnie

Instagram @marniejurkowski_qhht

Facebook Marnie Jurkowski QHHT

For updates on books and QHHT www.marniejurkowski.com

Email marniejurkowskiqhht@gmail.com

Meet Andy

Hey everyone, I want to share some of my journey and what I've learned. Living with autism and anxiety can be challenging, but you're not alone, and our struggles don't make us any less valuable. Music has been my lifeline, especially Korn's, which helped me through dark times and inspired me to write my own songs as therapy. I hope to be in a band one day, to help others through music as it helped me. Life does get better, even if it takes time. Healing is possible, and reaching out for help is always the right choice.

www.ingramcontent.com/pod-product-compliance
Lightning Source LLC
Chambersburg PA
CBHW052115030426
42335CB00025B/2997